CREATE
IN ME
A HEART
OF
WISDOM

Other Books from the (in)courage Community

DEVOTIONALS

Take Heart: 100 Devotions to Seeing God When Life's Not Okay

Empowered: More of Him for All of You

TRADE BOOKS

The Simple Difference by Becky Keife

Come Sit with Me

BIBLE STUDIES

Courageous Simplicity: Abide in the Simple Abundance of Jesus

Courageous Joy: Delight in God through Every Season

Courageous Influence: Embrace the Way God Made You for Impact

Courageous Kindness: Live the Simple Difference Right Where You Are

Create in Me a Heart of Hope

Create in Me a Heart of Peace

Create in Me a Heart of Wisdom

Create in Me a Heart of Mercy (available May 2023)

For more resources, visit incourage.me

AN
(in)courage
BIBLE STUDY

CREATE IN ME A HEART OF WISDOM

Grace P. Cho and the
(in)courage community

Revell
a division of Baker Publishing Group
Grand Rapids, Michigan

Published by Revell
a division of Baker Publishing Group
PO Box 6287, Grand Rapids, MI 49516-6287
www.revellbooks.com

Printed in the United States of America

Library of Congress Cataloging-in-Publication Data
Names: (in)courage (Organisation)
Title: Create in me a heart of wisdom / (in)courage.
Description: Grand Rapids, MI : Revell, a division of Baker Publishing Group, [2022] |
    Includes bibliographical references.
Identifiers: LCCN 2022006580 | ISBN 9780800738136 (paperback) | ISBN 9781493436248
    (ebook)
Subjects: LCSH: Wisdom—Biblical teaching—Textbooks.
Classification: LCC BS680.W6 C74 2022 | DDC 220.1—dc23/eng/20220711
LC record available at https://lccn.loc.gov/2022006580

23 24 25 26 27 28 29   7 6 5 4 3 2 1

CONTENTS

INTRODUCTION

We all want and need wisdom, but how do we get it?

When we're in a relationship with a toxic person and need boundaries, when our churches are divided by theological differences, when we don't know how to navigate unexpected difficulties, knowing what the right, good, or wise thing to do is difficult. It would be easier if wisdom were formulaic and we could follow a set of rules to fix every tricky situation.

But the wisdom we need is the kind that can guide us when there is no right answer, when choosing the best thing goes against our loved ones' advice, and when it seems impossible to find a way through complicated feelings, relationships, and circumstances. We need wisdom to live life fully, and that wisdom comes from God. He understands our realities, sees beyond what we can see, and is the ultimate source of knowledge and understanding. In Christ, we have access to God's wisdom through the Holy Spirit, who directs our steps and dwells within us.

Create in Me a Heart of Wisdom teaches that wisdom is learned by understanding knowledge, listening to the Holy Spirit, experiencing struggle, being in community, and practicing what we learn over a lifetime. It won't offer solutions to specific problems, but it will offer spiritual insight and practical guided questions throughout the study to help you seek God and gain the wisdom you need.

Over the next six weeks, discover the wisdom that is available to you when you ask God for it, and learn to walk wisely by the help of the Holy Spirit.

How to Use This Study

Create in Me a Heart of Wisdom is designed to be used by individuals or small groups. For groups doing this study, we recommend allowing at least forty-five minutes for discussion (or more for larger groups).

As you work through this study, take your time. Sit with the truths of God's Word and wrestle through what you're not sure about. If you feel challenged or you don't understand something, ask God to reveal His insight to you through the Holy Spirit.

This study is a guide to help you along your journey to becoming wise. It's not a prescribed path, so work at your own pace. If you don't get to every question or you want to linger longer in one week than another, that's okay! God can and will meet you, whether you spend thirty intentional minutes each day or you find moments here and there throughout the day.

Enhance your community study experience with our leader guide. Go to www .incourage.me/leaderguides to download your free small group resources.

Each week of this study will begin with a personal story from an (in)courage writer about how she learned wisdom through difficult life circumstances, through her community, or through faithful practice. Each week will also provide a memory verse (or verses) to work on throughout the study, to ground yourself in God's Word, and to come back to even after you finish this book. Make sure to have a Bible or Bible app on hand for reading Scripture, and if it helps to write things down, use a journal or index cards to write each week's memory verses.

The first day of each week will focus on the personal story and introduce the memory verse, and the following four days will explore how wisdom is learned, how to apply it, and the difference it can make in your life and the lives of those around you.

Are you ready? God wants to create in you a heart of wisdom, and we, your sisters at (in)courage, are right there with you in learning to become wise. Let's take a deep breath together and start the journey.

WISDOM IS LEARNED THROUGH UNDERSTANDING KNOWLEDGE

When we think of the word *wisdom*, we might think of sages, gurus, and experts—those who know the most about their subject of interest or who have mastered skills far beyond their peers. Or we might think of our grandparents, teachers, and mentors—those with more experience who have lived longer than us. As we mature in life and faith, we desire to become wise like them, but it's not always clear how to get there.

We often assume that wisdom will come naturally with age or with the accumulation of knowledge, but neither is 100 percent true. We can get along in years or stockpile facts about everything under the sun and still not be wise. So we must look to the one who started it all from the very beginning of time and ask Him to teach us what we need to know and help us understand it.

Today, I share a story about a time in my life when I thought (and was taught) that gaining knowledge would be my ticket into heaven. But knowledge by itself means nothing if we have no understanding behind it. As you read the story, think about how learning to understand knowledge is a path to wisdom.

A Story of Learning Wisdom

I held the small catechism book in my lap and traced the letters of its title with my fingertips. The bumpy texture of the cardstock cover reminded me of the feel of braille, and I pleaded with God that the words

I had obediently highlighted in pink would help me see the truth. I kept my thumb on the first page, constantly flipping the booklet open and closed because the wording of each question and answer was awkward. My mind struggled to understand how these words were supposed to help me in my faith, so I simply strung them together side by side, like a puzzle I'd understand when all the pieces were snapped together at the end. I repeated the questions and answers over and over again, like a prayer that could get me to heaven:

> Q.1. What is man's primary purpose?
>   A. Man's primary purpose is to glorify God and to enjoy him forever.
>
> Q.2. What does the Bible primarily teach?
>   A. The Bible primarily teaches what man must believe about God and what God requires of man.
>
> Q.3. What is God?
>   A. God is a Spirit, Whose being, wisdom, power, holiness, justice, goodness, and truth are infinite, eternal, and unchangeable.[1]

Instead of learning who God is behind these theological concepts, I simply committed the words to memory through repetition, knowing I'd only be asked to recite them correctly in Sunday school—not to understand them.

This was my spiritual education in my youth group and college days, gathering and hoarding knowledge, learning about white European theologians and their ideas from my Korean American pastors and Bible study teachers. I learned to build a case for my faith lest there come a time when other Christians who didn't believe the same way I did questioned my knowledge. And eventually, like a sheep without a shepherd, I regurgitated what I knew and fed it to the youth group students who came after me, faithfully following in the footsteps of those before me.

My prematurely formed theological knowledge became the foundation on which all my beliefs were grounded. It was the soapbox on which I'd stand to look down on anyone I deemed unenlightened. It was proof that I was wiser than my peers, who had the audacity not to care. It became the ten-foot pole I used to measure people's worthiness, including my own, and I was thoroughly disappointed in all of us whenever we didn't meet the standard.

I remember the intensity of those days and how exhilarating and powerful it felt to know so much. Even now I can almost smell the acidity of the thick paper from that sturdy little booklet, and I can instinctually recite what the chief end of man is. I was shaped by those catechisms, by the teaching and culture of my church at that time. And while I'm grateful for what I was taught and for the pastors and teachers who passed on that knowledge to me, I've come to realize that not everything I learned was good and right or even true. I've had to live through the consequences and take responsibility for the ways that ingested theology shaped the way I saw myself, how I treated others, and what I thought about the rest of the world.

My theology has changed and expanded, re-formed again and again over the years. I've learned to sift through everything I was taught, to examine it in sober judgment and see if it holds true not just for the elite but for everyone. I've learned that knowledge without understanding builds a flat, often unlived faith that lacks nuance and grace for self and others. And though knowledge can be good in and of itself, I've learned that the way we use it, why we believe it, and how we live it are what can lead to wisdom.

Recently, my husband and I bought and set up three bookshelves in our room to better organize the (possibly unnecessary) plethora of books we've accumulated over our lives. I began the satisfying work of sorting them, perfectly lining up the spines in just the right way, and tossing the ones I didn't need anymore into a donation box. When I got to the stack of books I had read during those formative years growing up, I paused. I thought about the ways they had been both helpful and harmful and how much fuller my library had become since I had read them.

I decided to keep them on their own shelf as a reminder of where I'd come from while acknowledging that so much of life and faith isn't clear-cut and categorical the way I'd thought it was. Instead of spouting knowledge as a way to position myself, I now try to take things in more mindfully, chewing on the information slowly and deliberately, seeking to understand more deeply. I've become comfortable with telling people, "I really don't know the answer," and letting uncertainty hang in the air. I trust that wisdom will come not because I amass knowledge but because God will help me understand what I need to learn.

—GRACE P. CHO

In what ways have you been taught to prize the accumulation of knowledge as a significant part of faith?

Read Proverbs 2:1–6. How does understanding lead to true knowledge and wisdom?

Look up 1 Corinthians 13:2. What does Paul say we are if we have knowledge but no love? What does this tell you about gaining knowledge without understanding it in a transformative way?

SCRIPTURE MEMORY MOMENT

This week's memory verse is Proverbs 2:6. Write the verse in your journal or on an index card (from the NIV as printed here or from your favorite translation). Throughout the week, commit these words to memory and ask God to create in you a heart of wisdom as you seek to understand the knowledge you learn.

For the LORD gives wisdom;
from his mouth come knowledge and
understanding.

A PRAYER FOR TODAY

GOD, *thank You for not expecting me to know everything in order to know You. But I also recognize that in order to know You, I need to understand more. Help me digest what I read in Your Word and what I learn about You from others through books, sermons, podcasts, or my community. Let what needs to sink in, sink in, and let everything else float away according to Your wisdom for my life. Amen.*

The heart of the discerning acquires knowledge,
  for the ears of the wise seek it out.

Proverbs 18:15

How does knowing more about God, yourself, and others give you wisdom for life?

_____

_____

_____

_____

Knowledge without understanding doesn't build a well-grounded faith, but we still need knowledge to grow in wisdom. They go hand in hand. Knowing more about God, ourselves, and others helps form a deeper understanding of each. When we see ourselves reflected in another person's face and stories, we're humbly reminded that we, too, are flesh and blood, made in God's image and therefore deserving of love and dignity just like everyone else. And when we understand the depth of God's sacrificial love for humanity, we can learn how to love others as He loved us. When we spend time with people who have different family backgrounds, cultural customs, and church traditions, we get to experience a broader view of God's multifaceted nature and creativity (more about this in week 4).

Let's start with knowing more about God. He is bigger than we can imagine and more mysterious than we can fathom, and to cover every aspect of His character would fill entire libraries of books and still not be enough. We'll never exhaust our knowledge of God, because our limited perspective and time can give us only a glimpse of who He is. So where do we begin?

In John 17:26, Jesus prays, "I have made you known to them, and will continue to make you known in order that the love you have for me may be in them and that I myself may be in them." Jesus, as God embodied in human form, reveals to us who God is through His life, death, and resurrection. Of course, all Scripture points to God, but we get the clearest picture of who God is through the life of Christ.

> **Read through John 1:1–14 two times. Pay attention to how John refers to Jesus as "the Word" and to what verses 1–4 and 14 particularly say about the Word. Why do you think it was necessary for Jesus to "make His dwelling among us" so we can know God?**

As God incarnate, Jesus displayed various aspects of God during His ministry. He makes seven of them explicit in His "I am" statements. Look up the following passages, finish the "I am" statements, and write down what you learned about God through them.

1. Read John 6:25–40.

   I am _____

   I learned _____

2. Read John 8:12.

   I am _____

   I learned _____

3. Read John 10:1–10.

   I am _____

   I learned _____

4. Read John 10:11–18.

   I am _____

   I learned _____

5. Read John 11:17–44.

   I am _____

   I learned _____

6. Read John 14:1–7.

   I am _____

   I learned _____

7. Read John 15:1–8.

   I am _____

   I learned _____

> ### The more we understand who God is, we can't help but be in awe that He is the one who loves us.

This is only scratching the surface of who God is! Scripture also tells us God is just, righteous, compassionate, empathetic, loving, gracious, holy, slow to anger, patient, faithful, unchanging, and wise. The list can go on and on, but as the apostle John writes at the end of his book, "Jesus did many other things as well. If every one of them were written down, I suppose that even the whole world would not have room for the books that would be written" (John 21:25).

Likewise, no matter how many Bible studies are written about God or any of His attributes, none of them—not even all of them together—can fully encapsulate who He is and what He has done. We cannot pin Him down or box Him in. He is magnificent, unbound, and so, so good. The more we understand who God is, we can't help but be in awe that He is the one who loves us.

Now let's read 1 Corinthians 8:3 and Galatians 4:9. What does it mean to you to be known by God? How does that feel?

_____

_____

_____

_____

When we begin to grasp the astounding nature of God, we see how significant it is not only that He loves us but that we are known by Him. The wonder of being known by a loved one is being fully seen for who we are—every little quirk, ache, and joy—and being accepted and celebrated. To be known is to be at home, to be at peace, to feel safe to simply be.

God is that person for us. He knows us completely and loves us whole-heartedly. But more often than not, we don't know or love ourselves as we ought to, as we *need* to. When this happens, we cannot be fully known by others. We can take it further to say that because God shows Himself through each of us, there will be some aspects of Him that we and others around us can't experience when we don't know ourselves.

A lack of self-awareness leads to choices that hurt instead of help—for us and for others. It can lead to confusion about purpose and passion or even about what we enjoy doing for fun. It can result in a lack of boundaries or finding our worth in the wrong places in the wrong way. A life lived not knowing ourselves is ultimately an unwise, unfulfilling life.

We are complex beings, with personalities, desires, traumas, love languages, pains, and fears, and we are constantly changing and growing. Though God knew who we'd become even before He knit us together in our mothers' wombs, we need to take the time to get to know ourselves.

If you need a place to begin, start with some personality tests, such as the Myers-Briggs Type Indicator, the Enneagram Type Indicator, or StrengthsFinder. You can also explore the Five Love Languages to understand how you give and receive love, and as a simple way to begin to know your own desires (the way you find joy and purpose), you can create a list—as long as you want—of things you want to do in life.[2]

These are simply tools and not the answers to all of life's questions. Some might be more helpful than others, and some might not work for you at all. If possible, seeking therapy and/or spiritual direction can be tremendously helpful in knowing yourself as well.

But let's be honest, this is hard work. Knowing, healing, and growing take time and energy, and sometimes it can feel like ignorance *is* bliss. It's easier to blame everyone else for our problems and issues with people. It might even feel like the right or peaceful choice would be to ignore our painful past and move on like nothing happened. But wisdom doesn't come from ignoring or suppressing or pretending. Wisdom comes as we intentionally take the steps to know ourselves and God.

> **Reflect on Proverbs 2:9–11. How does knowledge of God and self help and protect you?**

_____

_____

_____

_____

SCRIPTURE MEMORY MOMENT

Write out Proverbs 2:6. In what areas of your life do you need wisdom, knowledge, and understanding?

A PRAYER FOR TODAY

LORD, *thank You for not being far off or inaccessible but for being Immanuel, God with us and near us. Teach me how to know You through Your Word, through what I read and listen to, through other people, and even through what I'm learning about myself. I know I can't do this alone, and I'm a little scared that I might learn something terrible or disappointing about You or me. Give me courage to see and know who You are and who I am, and guide me to wisdom. Amen.*

The LORD brought me forth as the first of his works,
before his deeds of old;
I was formed long ages ago,
at the very beginning, when the world came to be.

Proverbs 8:22–23

Who or what is your go-to source for wise advice and why?

_____

_____

_____

_____

Raise your hand if you reach for your phone, open up a browser, and ask Google for the answer to every question you have. Whether we're searching for solutions to everyday problems, like how to unclog a sink drain, or searching for answers to more serious matters, like what side effects are caused by a parent's cancer medication, the internet has become our source of help, hope, knowledge, and wisdom. First of all, let's thank God for access to such a wealth of information! But then let's ask ourselves, How often do we turn to Google instead of God for wisdom?

I'm raising my hand right there with you! It's easy to turn to every other reliable source out there when we need guidance in understanding something. Trusting what's tangible is simpler than having faith in the unseen—and sometimes that's okay! God has given us tools, resources, friends, and mentors to help us live well, but we want to make sure that our ultimate source of understanding knowledge is the wisdom of God.

The Bible consists of sixty-six books written by various authors and in different genres. One genre is wisdom literature, which includes Job, Proverbs, and Ecclesiastes. Together, these books share practical insight on how to live wisely.

In Proverbs 8:1–9, God's wisdom is personified as a woman who stands at the city gates and urges us to listen and heed her call. Let's take a deep breath, settle in, and listen to what she has to say to us today.

Read Proverbs 8 in its entirety. What parts stand out to you about wisdom and why?

Let's focus on Proverbs 8:2–4. What do these verses tell you about wisdom's accessibility based on where she positions herself and who she calls to?

Wisdom offers herself fully, freely, and generously to anyone who will listen and choose her—regardless of our beliefs, status, life experiences, or background. And whether we're aware of it or not, wisdom is applied by people every single day in all spheres of life—whether it's by kings and rulers, as verses 15–16 tell us, or by the special needs teacher who's figuring out how to care for and educate her students well, or by the employee who wants to hold their manager accountable for inappropriate behavior, or by the young woman who notices the toxic behavior of a friend and doesn't know what to do. Everyone needs wisdom to live this life well.

For each sticky situation we find ourselves in and for all the knowledge we need help understanding, we have access to the ultimate source of insight we need: the wisdom of God.

And gaining wisdom is like gaining a friend who brings the best foods to the potluck! With wisdom we also get prudence, knowledge, and discretion (v. 12), along with counsel, sound judgment, insight, and power (v. 14)—a powerhouse combo of everything we need when we don't know what to do or say, when we're having a hard time understanding what we're going through, and when we're confused about how to handle delicate relationships or what the next step for our careers should be. Wisdom promises, "I love those who love me, and those who seek me find me" (v. 17).

> **What are some situations you're currently facing where you need wisdom? Write down as many as you can.**

God's wisdom is necessary for people to survive and flourish and fully enjoy life. His wisdom is our ultimate guide and has been since the very beginning of time. Thus, our passage for today:

> The LORD brought me forth as the first of his works,
>   before his deeds of old;
> I was formed long ages ago,
>   at the very beginning, when the world came to be.
>   (Prov. 8:22–23)

The wisdom of God created boundaries where there was formlessness, light where there was darkness, and order out of chaos. And as God delighted over each day's work, so did wisdom (v. 31).

Now, in the same way, wisdom continues the work of shaping and creating, ordering and delighting, and giving us life when we live according to her instructions. Better than Google, wisdom is accessible to all, giving us structure and guidelines by which we can thrive.

But living wisely doesn't mean that life will always be good or that we'll always be successful. From both Job and Ecclesiastes, we know that life can be full of ups and downs, circumstances that are out of our control, and times when the wicked prosper while the righteous suffer. And from our own experience, we know that life isn't fair or even guaranteed. Though wisdom teaches us the best way to live, sometimes things just don't work out the way we want them to.

When that happens (because it will), it doesn't mean you're not in the center of God's will or you're doing something wrong. Job's story is proof of that. Jesus says in John 16:33, "In this world you will have trouble." So, when the troubles come, wisdom is there to guide us back

Better than Google, wisdom is accessible to all, giving us structure and guidelines by which we can thrive.

to the source of all wisdom—God Himself. The book of Ecclesiastes ends with this reminder:

> Now all has been heard;
>   here is the conclusion of the matter:
> Fear God and keep his commandments,
>   for this is the duty of all mankind.
> For God will bring every deed into judgment,
>   including every hidden thing,
>   whether it is good or evil. (12:13-14)

It boils down to this: all we've got is God, and to begin to live wisely, we fear Him (Prov. 1:7) and obey His commandments. This doesn't mean we need to be afraid of Him. It means that we understand who He is and who we are—He is God, and we are not. We live, struggle through, and enjoy this one life we have while being in awe of Him. And we heed His words to us, choosing to walk in His love, grace, and wisdom.

Let's ask and seek God for wisdom, knowledge, and understanding because He is our greatest source for them all.

Let's end with Proverbs 8:32–36. What is the reward of listening to wisdom, and what is the consequence of not seeking wisdom?

_____

_____

_____

SCRIPTURE MEMORY MOMENT

Read and write out Proverbs 2:6 three times. Consider how this verse specifically states the source of wisdom.

A PRAYER FOR TODAY

GOD, *I love that from the very beginning of this world Your wisdom has been present, woven into everything we see and enjoy. I know nothing is guaranteed in life, even the goodness and well-being that could come with wisdom. But knowing that You are the source of all wisdom gives me confidence to navigate any situation. Even when there doesn't seem to be a way out, You can see a way through, and I trust You. I pray that my ears would be open to hear wisdom's call so that in everything I do, I can live wisely. Amen.*

But knowledge puffs up while love builds up.

1 Corinthians 8:1

When you think of people who are wise, what other characteristics do they have? How do they carry themselves and act toward others?

I shared a story this week of how I grew up in a very knowledge-focused church environment. I gained a solid foundation for my faith, but I didn't learn to steward or wield my knowledge wisely. Instead of living by grace alone, I used what I knew to earn my salvation and measure my worth, judging both myself and others.

Knowledge has power, and I think we inherently understand that we can use it for our own benefit or for the sake of others. First Corinthians 8:1 says that "knowledge puffs up while love builds up." In other words, knowledge for its own sake is meaningless, but knowledge applied wisely is love.

Yesterday we read the end of Ecclesiastes, which says,

> Now all has been heard;
>   here is the conclusion of the matter:
> Fear God and keep his commandments,
>   for this is the duty of all mankind. (12:13)

Solomon, who's traditionally believed to be the author of Ecclesiastes, is considered one of the wisest men to ever live. First Kings 4:29–30 says, "God gave Solomon wisdom and very great insight, and a breadth of understanding as measureless as the sand on the seashore. Solomon's wisdom was greater than the wisdom of all the people of the East, and greater than all the wisdom of Egypt."

Yet, he also lived foolishly, accumulating wealth and women and allowing his heart to be turned away from God (1 Kings 11:1–8). And after living a full life of experiencing wisdom, folly, riches, pleasures, and every privilege he could want, he concludes with this uncomplicated statement: "Fear God and keep his commandments" (Eccles. 12:13).

Could it really be that simple?

Read Mark 12:28–31. What does Jesus say is the most important commandment?

Living this truth might be hard and complicated, but it really *is* that simple! Knowledge applied wisely is love—loving God, loving others, and loving ourselves. As I shared in my story on day 1 of this week, it's what we do with knowledge and how we live it out that can lead to wisdom.

So, what do we do with the knowledge we gain? How do we know what is useful or helpful and what isn't? And how do we figure out how to wield it wisely? Write down some thoughts.

_____

_____

_____

_____

In 1 Corinthians 8, Paul begins by saying, "We know that 'We all possess knowledge.' But knowledge puffs up while love builds up. Those who think they know something do not yet know as they ought to know" (vv. 1–2). Paul goes on to teach that the discussion concerning food sacrificed to idols is not as black and white as it might seem. Knowledge—no matter how correct it may seem—can become a "resounding gong or a clanging cymbal" (1 Cor. 13:1) unless it's informed by love for our sister or brother.

That's a difficult truth to swallow! We might think, _If only everything could fall into neat categories and we had a formula to follow!_ But don't worry, we're not left to figure things out on our own. We have God's Spirit living within us and God's Word to guide us.

Knowledge applied wisely is love—loving God, loving others, and loving ourselves.

Based on the first two verses of 1 Corinthians 8, we can ask ourselves the following questions to help us wisely apply the knowledge we have:

1. Does my knowledge boost my self-worth and importance or does it build up and benefit those around me?
2. How's my heart as I hold this knowledge? Am I holding firmly, possibly stubbornly, to my need to be correct? Or am I willing to say that I don't know or even that I might be wrong?

Growing up, I thought that being right and knowing how to defend my faith were more important than loving the people who don't see things the way I do. I memorized Scripture, recited the catechism, and learned to say all the "right" things. But now I see: knowledge doesn't equate to faith or wisdom.

We need to take what we learn, sift it through God's Word and compare it to Jesus's life, and then do with it as His Spirit guides us—to build up in love.

Think back on what you've learned growing up—in the church, in your family of origin, or in your culture. What are some things that you now know aren't black and white or are completely wrong? How are you learning to wrestle it out with God?

We all carry baggage from our past, wounds we've endured and continue to endure, and tendencies and values that have been ingrained into us. We're pained people, working out our traumas, grief, and ignorance on one another, and at times it can seem impossible to know how to navigate difficult and delicate conversations and relationships—in person and online.

Furthermore, in a polarizing world, we're encouraged to take sides, to call the other the enemy, and to make gross and often unfair blanket statements about those who don't fully agree with us. We use what we know as a weapon against one another, shaping our words into machine guns that fire at will without wondering who it is we're shooting and if we should be shooting at all.

We are desperately in need of wisdom because we won't find easy answers for any of these problems. It would be too crude to force a general solution for what love should look like when every situation is more nuanced or complicated than we'd like it to be.

So we plead with God, asking Him to create in us a heart of wisdom. We hold our knowledge humbly and stay tender to the Spirit, trusting the Spirit will guide us. We recognize there will be times when we don't get it right, when we hurt others even though our intentions may be good, when we think we know enough but don't, and when we consciously act out of selfishness instead of love.

At such times, we repent, make things right where we can, and show grace to ourselves and others as we work toward love. We keep at it. This is work for the long haul as we grow to be wise.

Thank God for His wisdom that leads us each step of the way.

> **Read 1 Corinthians 13:1–3. Why is love so important in regard to wisdom, knowledge, and understanding?**

SCRIPTURE MEMORY MOMENT

Write out Proverbs 2:6. As you do, ask the Lord for wisdom, knowledge, and understanding.

A PRAYER FOR TODAY

GOD, *thank You that the greatest, most important commandment is simply to love. I confess I make it more complicated than it needs to be because I want to avoid doing the work of love. I'd rather use knowledge as a weapon to prove I'm right and defend myself, and if I'm being really honest, sometimes I want to use it to hurt and cut others down. Teach me to apply my knowledge to build others up, and create in me a heart of love and wisdom. Amen.*

The words of the reckless pierce like swords,
but the tongue of the wise brings healing.
Proverbs 12:18

When have you experienced the healing or destructive power of someone's words?

When we can hide behind our phones or computer screens, when a slip of the tongue can spread gossip like wildfire but keep us anonymous, when we can get others riled up in a comment thread for our own agenda, it's easier to pretend that our words won't hurt people too much. We might have defensible reasons or the right knowledge ready at the tip of our tongue, but as a wise friend once said, "You don't have to be a jerk about it."

As we've learned this week, knowledge is power, and how we wield it marks the difference between life or death, flourishing or destruction, selfishness or love. We use our words to make this choice multiple times a day—through texts, emails, the occasional phone call, or face-to-face conversation. We may not see their immediate impact, but as our words settle into the minds and hearts of real people, there can be echoing effects—for better or worse.

Throughout the Bible, we read that our mouth, lips, tongue, and words can bring forth wisdom or foolishness. They are the megaphones of our hearts, revealing what's inside. In Luke 6:45, Jesus says, "A good man brings good things out of the good stored up in his heart, and an evil man brings evil things out of the evil stored up in his heart. For the mouth speaks what the heart is full of."

As we explore the truths God has for us today, let's be honest with ourselves and with Him. Confess when you feel convicted, and feel free to use the margins of the pages to write out those confessions. Remember, conviction doesn't mean condemnation. Wisdom wants to teach us so we can grow, not to shame us.

> **Look up the following passages and write down what they say about the use and power of our words:**
>
> Proverbs 15:1   Proverbs 18:13   James 3:3–6
>
> Proverbs 16:24   Proverbs 18:21
>
> **How is self-control related to wisdom and how we wield our knowledge?**

In James 3:5–6, the author warns that the tongue, though a small part of the body, has the power to set the course of one's life—in this case, to set it on fire. It might sound extreme, but let's consider the illustration James uses of a great forest being set on fire by a small spark.

On September 5, 2020, a gender reveal party in Yucaipa, California, went haywire when a smoke-generating pyrotechnic device set fire to nearby grass. Over the next few weeks, the fire burned more than 22,000 acres of land, took the life of one firefighter, and injured several others—the devastating result of a seemingly harmless spark.[3]

Likewise, "the tongue"—our words—can cause damage when we don't use it wisely. James takes it further to say, "All kinds of animals, birds, reptiles and sea creatures are being tamed and have been tamed by mankind, but no human being can tame the tongue. It is a restless evil, full of deadly poison" (3:7–8).

It seems hopeless, doesn't it? If we can't tame the tongue, how do we use our words wisely? Wisdom teaches us how.

- **Take a second before you speak.** Proverbs 18:13 says, "To answer before listening—that is folly and shame." We live in a culture where reacting as quickly as possible is expected and praised. Taking your time to think twice, to cultivate an authentic and honest response, and to ask whether you even need to respond feels like a luxury instead of a necessity. Wisdom, however, invites us to take a beat, mull it over, and consult the Holy Spirit before we use our words.

- **What are you saying?** Our verse for today in Proverbs 12:18 says, "The words of the reckless pierce like swords, but the tongue of the wise brings healing." Will the words that are about to come out of your mouth tear down someone's humanity or dignity? Will they flatter instead of tell the truth? Will they bring healing or rub salt in the wounds of those who hear them? Wisdom invites us to examine our words, our jokes, our "Oh, I didn't mean it that way" phrases before they leave our mouth.

- **Do you need to say it?** Proverbs 17:27–28 says, "The one who has knowledge uses words with restraint, and whoever has

> Wisdom invites us to examine our words, our jokes, our "Oh, I didn't mean it that way" phrases before they leave our mouth.

understanding is even-tempered. Even fools are thought wise if they keep silent, and discerning if they hold their tongues." Sometimes we just don't need to say anything. Our words or our knowledge may not be helpful at all, or our attitude and timing may be off. Wisdom invites us to read the room and know when to keep our mouth closed.

Self-control takes practice. The goal isn't perfection or to be tamed in such a way that we become docile. We're aiming for wisdom to use our words with precision and power.

Let's pause for a moment. What has God been revealing to you about the way you use your words? If you haven't yet, write a prayer of confession and repentance and ask God for a heart of wisdom. Here's a basic outline you can follow:

God,

I recognize/see/acknowledge that I [fill in the blank with what you're confessing]. I understand that when I do that, I [fill in the blank with the consequence of using your words in the way you do]. Help me to be aware of my thoughts, my motives, and my words. Teach me to be wise. In Jesus's name, amen.

When we use our words wisely, we walk in the way of wisdom and reflect God's wisdom, which brings life, order, and beauty to this world. Proverbs 15:4 says, "The tongue that heals is a tree of life, but a devious tongue breaks the spirit" (CSB). Healing words create a refuge of rest, of *selah*, for people. Under the cool shade of wisdom, our words or our silence give them a soft place to land and find respite for their souls. They can be safe to bring their whole selves into conversations with us or to simply sit together in stillness and peace.

Let's take wisdom's words to heart, grow as we go, and become women who use our knowledge and understanding to bring healing to the world.

> Perhaps you're ending this week wishing you had people who used their words to heal instead of harm you. Take some time to grieve this reality. Read Psalm 30 slowly, and write down what brings you comfort and healing.

SCRIPTURE MEMORY MOMENT

Test yourself on Proverbs 2:6. Try to say it out loud or write it from memory. As we move into the next week of our study, continue to reflect on these words.

A PRAYER FOR TODAY

LORD, *thank You for today's practical reminders of how to use my words wisely. I needed them! Will You remind me when I forget (because I will), and will You change me to be a person who brings healing through my words? I look to You for help and for grace as I learn the way of wisdom. Amen.*

WISDOM IS LEARNED THROUGH LISTENING

When we proverbially sit at someone's feet to glean from their wisdom, we pay attention and actively listen. We take mental or literal notes of every word shared. We stay attuned to their body language, their tone of voice, their facial expressions, and we learn from their stories and their lives. Likewise, as we seek to gain wisdom from God, we pay attention to how His Spirit moves, learning to discern His voice above everyone else's and listening and obeying what He says.

As we'll see in our opening story from (in)courage writer Kristen Strong, the Holy Spirit guides us in our relationships, teaches us to know which voices to listen to, and helps us figure out how to come to the right decision with peace. As you read Kristen's story, think about how learning to listen to the Spirit is a path to wisdom.

A Story of Learning Wisdom

I stared at my phone, blinked several times, and looked back to see if I'd imagined the words. No, the stark sentences rose up from the phone like angled and curved little soldiers, marching right over my stunned, shattered heart.

My husband, David, seeing the shocked look on my face, asked me what was wrong. I handed the phone to him and collapsed onto the living room sofa.

"Am I being sensitive or is this ridiculously ugly?" I asked him in a shaky voice.

As he read the message, his eyes widened and he shook his head back and forth. He set the phone down hard on the end table next to me and said, "This is utter garbage, and I don't think you have any business communicating further with this person. *At all.*"

In general, I'm one who doesn't like conflict. While I'm capable of standing up for myself, some people's strong personalities make me less inclined to do so. In situations like these, I lean toward wanting to smooth things over as quickly as possible. At the same time, I was so tired of the way this person repeatedly put me on the defensive by being hypercritical of every choice I made.

Like a lost traveler smack-dab in the middle of a forest, I couldn't see how to take appropriate next steps to get out of the woods. Should I take my husband's advice and severely limit communication? But what about the fact that as a Christian I'm supposed to lay down my life for others and turn the other cheek?

Where is the line between having to spend time with difficult people we're called to be around and needing to protect our hearts and health from their toxicity?

In today's culture, it's somewhat trendy for people to label any kind of undesirable communication as toxic. This can give us a handy excuse to ignore sentiments we don't like. Of course, we *do* need people in our lives who offer us the gift of a painful rebuke from time to time. But their motive is what makes the difference—they are for us and not for themselves.

While we're sometimes called to be in the vicinity of difficult people as the Holy Spirit directs, we don't need to be in the vicinity of toxicity. Wisdom is found in knowing the difference. And wisdom is found in going to the right places for help in deciphering the distinction. After all, part of knowing where we belong is also knowing where we *don't*.

In John 14:16 Jesus says, "And I will ask the Father, and he will give you another Helper, to be with you forever" (ESV). The Holy Spirit is our forever Helper who informs us on a plethora of decisions, including how to maneuver difficult relationships. And sometimes the Holy Spirit will work through the voices of others to affirm what the Bible says.

In his stellar book *When to Walk Away*, author Gary Thomas lays out some characteristics of toxic people, including those who:

> Consistently add chaos to your life.
>
> Don't simply disagree with you but try to silence you.
>
> Attempt to stop you from doing or being what God has called you to do or be.
>
> Zap your strength and hurt your health.[1]

In short, the wisdom we seek in dealing with toxic people should point toward a measure of order, not further the chaos. The actions stemming from that wisdom should be motivated by love. And as I thought about my relational patterns with this particular difficult person, it seemed that the best way to love him was to set boundaries that were as much for him as they were for me.

If you struggle to take my word for it, then take Jesus's word on the importance of establishing boundaries. He either walked away from people or let people walk away from Him over two dozen times in the four Gospels.[2] One such time is described in Matthew 12:14–15: "But the Pharisees went out and plotted how they might kill Jesus. Aware of this, Jesus withdrew from that place."

Yes, when the time came for God's redemptive plan to be fulfilled, Jesus did suffer and die for us. But He followed His Father's direction—not other people's—on when that would happen.

Jesus knew where He belonged, and He also knew where He did not belong. He used His Father's guidance to direct His steps and to erect appropriate boundaries in each situation. And Jesus knew something we all need to remember:

Sometimes being on the outside is the healthiest place to be.

David and I once again discussed his earlier advice, which indeed reflected Scripture. Also, David is a levelheaded, emotionally even-keeled fellow. If he advised me to take bigger measures to limit my communication with this person, I knew he wasn't being dramatic or over-the-top. He was being wise.

So I set boundaries. And while that was one of the hardest things I've had to do, it was also one of the most freeing. With wisdom found in Scripture through the direction of the Holy Spirit and validated through the voice of my husband, I had peace that setting these boundaries was the right decision.

And I could see how being on the outside of that relationship put me further inside God's wise care and protection—the healthiest place to be.

—**KRISTEN STRONG**

In situations of conflict, whose voice is loudest to you and to whom do you listen the most?

Read John 10:2–4. Why is it important to know what God's voice sounds like?

Look up Proverbs 1:5. What posture do we need to have in order to listen?

SCRIPTURE MEMORY MOMENT

This week's memory verse is John 14:26. Write the verse in your journal or on an index card (from the NIV as printed here or from your favorite translation). Throughout the week, commit these words to memory and ask God to create in you a heart of wisdom as you learn to listen to the Holy Spirit.

But the Advocate, the Holy Spirit, whom the Father will send in my name, will teach you all things and will remind you of everything I have said to you.

A PRAYER FOR TODAY

GOD, *thank You for the Holy Spirit. Thank You that You are Immanuel, God with us, because even now Your Spirit lives within us. As I learn to listen this week, help me to know Your voice and be able to discern it from the many others around me. Holy Spirit, I receive Your teaching and guidance this week. Amen.*

DAY 2

For who knows a person's thoughts except their own spirit within them? In the same way no one knows the thoughts of God except the Spirit of God. What we have received is not the spirit of the world, but the Spirit who is from God, so that we may understand what God has freely given us.

1 Corinthians 2:11–12

Look up the word *discern* in the dictionary. How is discernment related to wisdom? Why is it necessary that we learn to discern spiritually?

Most days we spend our time unaware that we are spiritual beings living in both a physical and spiritual reality. Our mundane routines, full schedules, and mind-consuming problems keep our eyes focused on what's physically right in front of us. When there's so much to take care of and do, it might seem too mystical or disconnected from reality to consider anything that lies beyond our tangible needs. But the physical and spiritual coincide and overlap, and we need to live mindful of both; wisdom requires that we do.

In Ephesians 6:12, Paul says, "For our struggle is not against flesh and blood, but against the rulers, against the authorities, against the powers of this dark world and against the spiritual forces of evil in the heavenly realms." Understanding this, we learn to distinguish God's voice and what might be happening in the spiritual realm without overspiritualizing everything in our lives.

This might feel overwhelming or seem complicated to you, and that's okay. Our faith is both mysterious and simple. Some things are easy to comprehend and practice, and other things feel like taking a shot in the dark. But God is not a far-off deity who relishes keeping us in confusion and at arm's length. He is Immanuel, God with us and near us.

> **Look up 1 Corinthians 3:16. What does this passage tell you about the nearness of God through the Holy Spirit?**

> **Read Matthew 10:5–20. What do you think it means to be "as shrewd as snakes"?**

When we have the Spirit of God within us, we learn how to discern what feels elusive and difficult. Discernment isn't a spiritual moment where you say a prayer and a magic bell dings, giving you clarity in the moment. Instead, it is being in tune with who God the Spirit is, understanding how He moves, and learning to go where He leads.

In John 3:8, Jesus tells Nicodemus, "The wind blows wherever it pleases. You hear its sound, but you cannot tell where it comes from or where it is going. So it is with everyone born of the Spirit." Throughout Scripture the Hebrew and Greek words used for "breath" and "wind"— *ruach* and *pneuma*, respectively—are also used for "spirit," and specifically in reference to the Holy Spirit.[3] Just as wind swirls in and around, fluttering leaves or causing tornadoes, the Spirit of God is invisible but powerful. He is a felt presence, whose impact we can see because of the change He effects on people.

Being in tune with the Spirit means that we follow His lead. In a dance, one person leads and the other follows, and when the two are in sync, the dance is seamless, fluid, and breathtaking. We come to know how the Spirit moves by learning what God reveals to us in Scripture and through the stories and testimonies of the church and its people. At the same time, we leave our understanding open-ended, knowing that the Spirit moves freely and boundlessly.

So when Jesus encourages His disciples to be as "shrewd as snakes" (Matt. 10:16), the wisdom He shares is for us to move as the Spirit moves. To be shrewd means to be clever, astute, and sharp. A snake can find ways in and out of rocks and hard places, and in Scripture, its wiliness is mostly seen as deceitful or cunning. But in the positive way Jesus uses it, shrewdness is the wisdom we need when there's no right answer to a situation or when we need to walk the fine line in complicated relationships. It's the keen ability to sense in our gut or spirit that something is off with certain people or in particular situations and knowing who is or isn't a person of peace (10:13). Shrewdness means

Being in tune with the Spirit means that we follow His lead.

being subtle when needed, alert to what's happening around us, flexible and ready to move as the Spirit moves.

On the other side of shrewdness is the wisdom of being "innocent as doves" (10:16). We don't use our insight against people or for our own benefit; our keenness is not to be manipulative. The Holy Spirit will never lead us to malign or disparage others with our words or actions. Being wise means being both "shrewd as snakes" and "innocent as doves," and by keeping in step with the Spirit, we can discern with integrity what each situation calls for.

> Moving as the Spirit moves might sound vague, so let's study the following passages in their contexts. Write down what happens when the Spirit moves and when we're filled with the Spirit.
>
> Genesis 1:2
>
> John 16:13–14
>
> Acts 1:8 with Acts 2:2–4
>
> Romans 8:6
>
> Galatians 5:22–26

Our Scripture passage for today says that "no one knows the thoughts of God except the Spirit of God" and that since we received the Spirit of God, "we may understand what God has freely given us" (1 Cor. 2:11–12). The passage goes on to say that "the person without the Spirit does not accept the things that come from the Spirit of God but considers them foolishness, and cannot understand them because they are discerned only through the Spirit" (v. 14). We need the Spirit to understand God and to listen and accept His words to us, to be able to discern God's wisdom and not consider it foolishness.

In John 3, Jesus explains to Nicodemus that one must be born again of water and the Spirit to enter the kingdom of God: "Flesh gives birth to flesh, but the Spirit gives birth to spirit" (v. 6). Nicodemus, a Pharisee and member of the Jewish ruling council—someone who should understand what Jesus is saying—doesn't get it. Jesus continues His monologue, saying,

> No one has ever gone into heaven except the one who came from heaven—the Son of Man. Just as Moses lifted up the snake in the wilderness, so the Son of Man must be lifted up, that everyone who believes may have eternal life in him. For God so loved the world that he gave his one and only Son, that whoever believes in him shall not perish but have eternal life. For God did not send his Son into the world to condemn the world, but to save the world through him. (vv. 13–17)

Did the Spirit move in Nicodemus for him to understand, to believe? In John 7:50–52 we read that Nicodemus subtly speaks up for Jesus, questioning his fellow leaders who want to seize Him. And later, after Jesus is crucified, Nicodemus accompanies Joseph of Arimathea to care for and properly prepare Jesus's body for burial (John 19:38–42).

The Bible may not explicitly say that Nicodemus believed, but we see evidence of the Spirit moving in him, leading him to truth, life, and love.

The Holy Spirit is moving, blowing like the wind. Let's pay attention and follow.

Read John 3:19–21. How do we recognize the Spirit in our lives and in the lives of others?

_____

_____

_____

_____

SCRIPTURE MEMORY MOMENT

Write out John 14:26. In what area of your life do you need the discernment and shrewdness of the Spirit?

A PRAYER FOR TODAY

LORD, _I need You even more than I realized. I can't know You without Your Spirit. Holy Spirit, lead me into truth. Teach me to walk in step with You. Give me a discerning heart to recognize You in my life, in the lives of others, and in the world as You move like the wind. Amen._

DAY 3

And I will ask the Father, and he will give you another advocate to help you and be with you forever—the Spirit of truth.

John 14:16–17

What do you know about the Holy Spirit and what has your experience been with the Spirit?

_____

_____

_____

_____

This week Kristen Strong shared a story about the wisdom of setting boundaries with a toxic person in her life. She listened to and trusted the voice of the Holy Spirit that spoke to her through Scripture and her husband's affirmation. She wasn't alone in making the hard decision to take healthy steps away from that person. She had the ultimate Helper to guide her through a difficult choice.

She quoted John 14:16 from the ESV, which says, "And I will ask the Father, and he will give you another Helper, to be with you forever." The Greek word translated as "Helper" is *paraklētos*, which can also mean counselor, comforter, advocate, intercessor, or one who comes alongside. As Jesus prepares to face His death and eventually leave His disciples, He promises another Helper to come and be with them—and now with us.

Does that phrase "with us" ring a bell? Jesus's birth story is recorded in the book of Matthew, where the Lord appears to Joseph in a dream and tells him, "'She [Mary] will give birth to a son, and you are to give him the name Jesus, because he will save his people from their sins.' All this took place to fulfill what the Lord had said through the prophet: 'The virgin will conceive and give birth to a son, and they will call him Immanuel' (which means 'God with us')" (Matt. 1:21–23).

Jesus *was* Immanuel. He was God with us, dwelling among us (John 1:14). And He promised to continue this with-ness through the Holy Spirit. In John 14:18 He says, "I will not leave you as orphans; I will come to you." God with us is now God who lives *within* us—the Holy Spirit.

> Read Isaiah 9:6. What is another name given to Jesus that connects to the Holy Spirit?
>
> _____
>
> _____
>
> _____
>
> _____
>
> Though the concept of God's three-person Trinity is too immense to fully understand, it's helpful to recognize that the Holy Spirit continues the

God with us is now God who lives within us—the Holy Spirit.

work of Jesus in us today. Look up our memory verse for this week (or recite it if you can). How does John 14:26 show this continued thread of work between Jesus and the Holy Spirit? (You can also compare John 16:13.)

_____

_____

_____

_____

The Holy Spirit is probably the least understood person in the Trinity. If your experience in the church was anything like mine growing up, you probably know little to nothing about the Spirit. That or you may have had negative or even pain-filled experiences where people have abused the gifts of the Spirit to manipulate and harm you.

You're not alone.

There's much to explore and learn about the Holy Spirit, and I hope what you learn this week will pique your curiosity so you continue expanding your understanding and experience of the Spirit beyond this study.

As my knowledge of God has evolved and expanded over time and as my faith has grown, the analogy of the wind has been the best way for me to grasp who the Spirit is, what He does, and how He moves.

For the last several months, whether due to climate change or simply a strange natural phenomenon, the wind will pick up every day in the late afternoon and start to blow through our area. At first, my family and I thought it was the change in seasons from winter to spring, but the pattern has continued as spring now turns into summer.

At the dinner table, one of us is bound to mention this curiosity because we're still surprised that the wind shows up without fail around the same time every single day. Its daily presence is a tangible reminder of the Spirit and Jesus's description in John 3:8: "The wind blows wherever it pleases. You hear its sound, but you cannot tell where it comes from or where it is going."

Every day the wind reminds us of God's invitation to be open to learning more while understanding less—this is the paradox of wisdom. As we know more about God and the Spirit, we see how vast and mysterious God is; He is beyond comprehension. So while we can learn more about God, the Spirit will not be harnessed and dissected into bite-size pieces of knowledge by our theoretical study. And just as the wind is unpredictable in its power or path, we cannot control whom or how the Spirit will move.

The invitation, then, is to come and see, to experience the Holy Spirit in our lives. We cannot be wise or live in power without Him.

> **Read Acts 2:1–13. What stands out to you in the Pentecost story regarding how the Holy Spirit came upon the people and the result of that?**

On the day of Pentecost, the Holy Spirit came like the sound of a violent wind and filled the house where the disciples, the women who followed Jesus, and His mother and brothers were gathered. What appeared like flames rested on them, and all of them were filled with the Holy Spirit and began speaking in other tongues. In an instant, the power of the Spirit was seen, heard, and experienced—not only by those in the house but also by the many Jews from far-off places who were staying in Jerusalem and heard the sound of their own languages being spoken.

This anointing of the Spirit is reminiscent of another. In Matthew 3:16, Jesus came out of the water after being baptized by John the Baptist, and the Spirit of God came down like a dove from heaven and rested on Him. Filled with the Spirit, Jesus was led into the desert to be tempted by Satan before beginning His years of ministry.

In both stories, the Spirit's work is evident—to empower those who are anointed and to change minds and hearts toward the truth.

This continues today. The Spirit, who anointed Jesus and came down like fire at Pentecost, is the same Spirit who dwells among us and in us. When we are filled with the Spirit, we are empowered to walk in wisdom, to listen to and obey God's voice, and to love as He first loved us (1 John 4:19).

Being Spirit-filled and anointed can look different for everyone. For some, it may be evident in how they pray in tongues or how they can speak truth into a person's life without knowing much about them. It can look like the gift of teaching and preaching God's Word in a way that convicts and softens the hardest of hearts. It can be seen through sketches and paintings and other creative mediums through which God's Spirit reveals the divine.

The Spirit moves like the wind, showing up at coffee shops, among those experiencing homelessness on the streets, inside church walls, and in the hallways of college dorms. He teaches those who are old through the mouths of little ones, and He shows us how to heal through the help of others.

The Spirit of God isn't a side character in the Trinity but is Immanuel— the one who walks right alongside us, guiding us and empowering us to live wisely. His nearness within us guarantees that we *can* have wisdom if we listen to His voice.

Open yourself up to the work of the Spirit. Be filled, anointed, and empowered.

> Read 1 Corinthians 12:4–11 and Galatians 5:16–26. What are some examples of Spirit-filled living?

SCRIPTURE MEMORY MOMENT

Read and write out John 14:26 three times. As you write, ask the Holy Spirit to help you understand His role in your faith and life.

A PRAYER FOR TODAY

HOLY SPIRIT, *come. So much of knowing You still feels unclear, but I want to know more. Teach me to distinguish Your voice from my own and to sense Your guidance in my gut. Give me the courage to follow You and the faith to trust You. Thank You for being my Advocate, my Helper, and my Wonderful Counselor. Amen.*

DAY 4

If you love me, keep my commands.

John 14:15

We've talked this week about gaining wisdom by listening to the Spirit. What does that mean to you on a practical level? What should listening lead us to do?

_____

_____

_____

_____

In any relationship we're in, we hope the other person listens with the intent of taking in our words and acting on them, so we feel known and understood. Listening that doesn't lead to action tells us that our words went in one ear and out the other. Eventually, no matter how good a person is at listening, if there's no consequent action we question whether their love for us is real.

The same goes for our relationship with God. Love will lead to action. James 1:22 says, "Do not merely listen to the word, and so deceive yourselves. Do what it says." We experience wisdom that comes from listening to the Spirit when we actually put into practice the words we hear from the Spirit. We become wise when we obey.

Easier said than done, right?

We may want wisdom. We might genuinely want to obey God because we love Him. But what happens when His direction seems to go against the logic and trusted advice of our community? What should we do when there seems to be more than one right answer or multiple paths we could take? What about the times when we obey but life doesn't work out the way we thought it would? What if obedience means giving up everything?

Obedience can feel like we don't have a choice, like a hardhanded way for God to make us do what He wants us to do. We might equate it to sacrifice and dying to self—two more ideas that create the impression that God only wants to use us. But His love for us doesn't hinge on our obedience. He loves us because He just does (John 3:16). And because He loves us, we love in return by obeying. Obedience, then, is love in action, and wisdom, therefore, is listening in action.

Read John 15:9–11. How is joy connected to obedience?

_____

_____

_____

_____

What does the word *obedience* bring up for you? What are some of your fears related to obedience?

_____

_____

_____

_____

It's natural that we'd balk at obedience when there's a cost to it. Self-preservation is a human reaction to protect ourselves from harm. But sometimes obedience will ask us to go beyond our comfort zones, and we'll need to make a choice: either trust and follow God, gaining wisdom and understanding, or not trust Him, stay where we are, and miss out on what God has for us on the other side of obedience. There's a cost either way, and we have to decide what we're willing to pay.

In Proverbs 8:10–11, wisdom tells us what she's worth:

> Choose my instruction instead of silver,
>   knowledge rather than choice gold,
> for wisdom is more precious than rubies,
>   and nothing you desire can compare with her.

Repeat that last phrase to yourself: "nothing you desire can compare with her."

But when the words we hear from the Holy Spirit make no sense for our lives or for the season we're in, it's difficult to remember that truth. Sometimes God leads us in a direction that seems so far from the path we were already on—a path He once led us to—that it throws us for a loop. We throw our hands up in frustration or anger, and we wonder, *What does this mean? How can this be? Why, God? Why?*

Once we can quiet our souls enough to be still, though, we weigh out what we know, what we're afraid of, what is truth, and which path is the way to wisdom. We can ask ourselves:

- What was it that God said to me? How has He been confirming it?
- What am I afraid of and why? What's not sitting right with me?
- Does Scripture say anything about what God is asking of me? What truth from Scripture counteracts my fears?
- Which way will lead to nearness with God and growth in wisdom?

> The Spirit *will* lead us to truth, and wisdom is obeying *even if.* Even if it doesn't make logical sense. Even if it looks like foolishness to others. Even if God is the only one who keeps confirming the same thing over and over again.

You might be able to answer these questions with clarity, or you might still feel confused, even after prayer and consulting others. Keep bringing it up to God in prayer and continue asking these questions. Gaining wisdom through listening and obeying is a process—one that becomes easier to decipher the more you practice.

Read John 16:12–15. What is the guarantee we find in these verses?

_____

_____

_____

_____

The Spirit *will* lead us to truth, and wisdom is obeying *even if*. Even if it doesn't make logical sense. Even if it looks like foolishness to others. Even if God is the only one who keeps confirming the same thing over and over again. Will you take steps to say yes to God, to trust Him, even if?

When I was in pastoral ministry, I had no dreams or plans to leave my job. I felt called to the church where I worked. I was happy to be serving people I cared for and content living in a city I had fallen in love with. I was fully committed to the work God was doing there and was ready to settle down, raise my family, and live the rest of my life right where I was.

But about six years into it, God began to close that chapter—both my time in ministry and our life as we knew it. He was redirecting us back home. I sat with this quietly for a year, unsure of what to make of it and with no concrete plans of what we were supposed to do next. It not only seemed like foolishness, but it felt backwards. We were moving in with my in-laws to live in the home my husband grew up in.

But God brought up the same messages of home and family again and again through that year of seeking wisdom. And even though our ducks weren't in a row before we moved, we knew in our gut that the timing was right, that God would be with us, and that He would show us each next step.

It's been five years now, and though I'm not any clearer on a five-year plan, I've come to the point where I don't need one anymore. God has again proven Himself trustworthy as always—through deep pits of depression, through painful moments in our marriage, and through the confusion of career changes for me and my husband.

Each yes has led to the next yes, and God's wisdom, God's Spirit, has been faithful to guide us in every "even if" and "even when."

And now I understand what John 15:11 means: God's joy has been in me, and my joy is full, complete—even if, even when.

What is something God is inviting you into that you need to obey?

SCRIPTURE MEMORY MOMENT

Write out John 14:26. As you do, ask the Holy Spirit to remind you of what God has said to you and to help you obey it.

A PRAYER FOR TODAY

LORD, *help me reframe my idea of obedience from one of dread and doom to one of love and joy. Thank You for the guarantee that Your Spirit will lead me to truth and to wisdom. Even when I can't see its worth, help me choose wisdom. Even if I look foolish to others, help me take steps toward saying yes to You. I want to experience the joy of obedience as I learn to become wise. Meet me where I am, God, and take me where You want me to be. Amen.*

DAY 5

This is what we speak, not in words taught us by human wisdom but in words taught by the Spirit, explaining spiritual realities with Spirit-taught words.

1 Corinthians 2:13

What is an insight that a wise person in your life has given you? It can be about God, yourself, or another person, or about a situation you were in.

_____

_____

_____

_____

Earlier this week we talked about recognizing that we live in a world that is both physical and spiritual. Both are equally part of who we are and the space in which we exist. They cannot be separated within us or around us. As we listen to the Spirit and tune in to God's voice, the wisdom we gain is spiritual. It helps us see beyond what's right in front of us and reaches into the hearts of those we speak to and are in relationship with.

Today we'll be unpacking the impact we can have with the wisdom we gain through listening—to both the Spirit and one another.

When I first began to sense God leading me into the work and ministry of writing, I doubted His direction and His knowledge of me. (Ridiculous, I know.) For several years I danced in and out of doubt and conviction. While God kept affirming that I should write, I couldn't get over the fact that no one had ever affirmed writing as a calling for my life instead of just a hobby project.

One day a friend sat me down, looked me in the eye, and said, "If you don't obey, other people will be missing out on the blessing they could receive through your obedience." She snapped me from my confusion and insecurity by sharing her wisdom and gave me the perspective I needed to stop wavering and start writing. Her words were a reminder that though my obedience was between me and God, the impact of my obedience could be wide.

All I could see was the humiliation of possible failure and the confusion of changing careers and passions, but my friend was able to cut through the fog and see that God was doing something new.

> In my story and in Kristen's story at the beginning of this week, we listened to the Spirit speak through trusted people in our lives. Who are those wise, trustworthy people in your life? Write down their names and thank God for each of them. If you don't have those kinds of people in your life, take a moment and ask God for them.

Read 1 Corinthians 2:14–16. What does this passage tell you about our ability to discern spiritually because we're in Christ?

_____

_____

_____

_____

We are blessed by wise people in our lives, and as we practice listening to the Spirit and walking in wisdom, we in turn bless others. We become fountains of understanding, knowledge, and insight, and people are refreshed in our presence, their weary souls sated. With words taught to us by the Spirit, we can help restore joy, heal pain, and guide others toward wisdom.

But first, in order to know what to say, we need to make sure we're multitasking in our listening. By that I mean we listen to the Spirit _as_ we listen to others tell us their stories, their struggles, their celebrations, and their prayer requests. We pay attention to repeated words or sentiments and take note of pain and vulnerability in their sharing. Then we ask God how we should respond, what we need to say, or if we should simply remain silent.

Let's say you meet a friend for coffee, and after catching up, she begins to vent to you about a relationship gone awry—again. You listen as she tells you about the latest scuffle and the continued misunderstanding between her and her coworker. You notice that the problem is just another version of the last conflict they had. The same feelings of frustration and hurt are repeated from before, and both parties feel they are in the right.

As you listen to her, you ask God what she might need right now. Is it simply a listening ear? What does she need to hear about God or herself? Is it time to show her the repeated patterns? If it's time, how can you approach the conversation so her ears stay open to hear God's wisdom through you? Or is she too stubborn and unable to hear anything constructive you have to say?

After sifting through and listening to how the Spirit is leading you, you follow through and see what happens. Sometimes you will say exactly what the person needs to hear, and other times you'll miss the mark. Or it might be that the other person isn't ready to hear what the Spirit wants to say to them. That's okay. Our obedience is simply to do as the Spirit guides us, and God will do the rest.

In Christ, we have the Spirit of God within us, and He empowers us to counsel and walk alongside others the way He does for us.

> **Look up Proverbs 16:20–21. How is wisdom necessary in a conversation for both the listener and the speaker?**

As we discern through the Holy Spirit and seek to guide others wisely, we need to remember the truth that we are not God. Therefore, there's always a chance we won't get it right. This might seem like a no-brainer, but in our desire to help, lead, and counsel, we can get ahead of ourselves and begin to make too much of our gift of wisdom.

Our obedience is simply to do as the Spirit guides us, and God will do the rest.

The same is true of the people we ask for wisdom: they are not God. In the church's current celebrity culture that makes idols of teachers, preachers, leaders, and other influencers, we're prone to trust and believe every word that comes from their mouths. Without thinking twice, we take their words as God's word to us.

Unfortunately, that sort of pattern sets everyone up for foolishness instead of wisdom. Whenever we receive wisdom from others, we need to take everything with a grain of salt and examine it for ourselves against God's Word. Also, when we are the ones guiding others, we must teach them to take our words with a grain of salt and to think for themselves as well. Yes, we can learn from one another, but ultimately we need to listen to the Spirit of God and guide others to do the same.

The grain of salt *is* wisdom.

As we end this week, let's continue to practice listening and speaking with wisdom taught by the Spirit. And let's bless and empower those around us to discern and live wisely too.

How have you mistaken other people's wisdom for God's without thinking twice? How can you make sure to take things in with a grain of salt from here on out?

SCRIPTURE MEMORY MOMENT

Test yourself on John 14:26. Try to say it out loud or write it from memory. As we move into the next week of our study, continue to reflect on these words.

A PRAYER FOR TODAY

GOD, *thank You for the Holy Spirit, who teaches me everything I need to learn and remember. Help me to distinguish between spiritual and human wisdom and to discern Your voice from others' voices. Help me be wise in what I take in and what I give out, and keep me humble in knowing that I am not You—what a relief! Guide us all by Your truth and by Your Spirit alone. Amen.*

WISDOM IS LEARNED THROUGH EXPERIENCE

Life guarantees that everyone will go through some sort of suffering. We can't control when or why it will happen or to whom. Life is unpredictable. Good-hearted, generous people will experience horrible things, and evil, selfish people will experience fortune and privilege. Ecclesiastes 9:11 says,

> I have seen something else under the sun:
> The race is not to the swift
>   or the battle to the strong,
> nor does food come to the wise
>   or wealth to the brilliant
>   or favor to the learned;
> but time and chance happen to them all.

When life happens to us, we don't have a choice but to learn wisdom the hard way. Faith takes on a whole new meaning when all we see is pain, and wisdom isn't a trophy we receive at the end. Instead, it's hard-won through the struggle as we seek to find God in the midst of it all.

You'll see so much of this to be true in our opening story from (in)courage writer Michele Cushatt. As you read it, consider how you can gain wisdom through unexpected, difficult, and painful experiences.

A Story of Learning Wisdom

It was during my middle school years that I first started praying for wisdom. I can't quite remember if it was a Sunday morning service or a message at a church camp, but the pastor preached a sermon on wisdom. Too many years have since passed for me to remember much else, but I do remember this: he said God promises to give wisdom to anyone who asks for it (James 1:5–6).

Call me an opportunist, but I wasn't about to pass up a sure thing, especially when it came to getting my prayers answered. I'd had enough unanswered prayers by that point to be curious about the legitimacy of a money-back Bible guarantee. It couldn't hurt to ask, right?

So that's when I started praying for wisdom—not just asking for King Solomon–sized portions of it but also giving thanks to God for what I was certain He would do. I believed James's words to be a black-and-white prescription. Thus, I gave thanks as I prayed, long before God had any time to make sure my prayer was answered. That's what faith does, right? I mustered my thirteen-year-old belief and determined to pray bold, believing prayers. Time would prove the pastor's words true. Or not.

It's now been well over thirty-five years since I began those wisdom-hungry prayers. As I reflect on the innocence of my request, I can't help but shake my head at both my audacity and naivete. I had no idea what I was asking or how our Father would choose to fulfill His promise.

At the time and for many years afterward, I thought God's wisdom-giving would come much like the bestowing of a magical power. Picture Tinker Bell waving her hand and sprinkling pixie dust, offering the receiver unexpected and sparkling flying powers. I liked the sound of that. And I was more than happy to have the Almighty wave His hand of divine wisdom in my direction.

Instead, by my midtwenties, I found myself entering into a season of consecutive losses and unrelenting suffering that wouldn't let up for decades. These sufferings included multiple painful ministries in three different states, miscarriage, divorce and single motherhood, remarriage and stepfamily, parenting adolescents through several tough years, a church split and multiple moves, foster and adoption of three more kids with a history of abuse and neglect, the death of my father from a thirteen-month battle with pancreatic cancer, and then three cancer diagnoses in four years that nearly cost me my life.

All of this before I turned forty-four years old.

Wisdom? What I needed was relief. Even with all this life experience, I didn't wake up one day as wise as Solomon. Instead, I spent months and years wrestling with my faith and the God I'd always loved. I scoured the pages of my Bible, trying to make sense of my suffering and explain my pain. I listened to podcasts and read books by pastors and theologians—dead and alive—who'd likewise suffered. I prayed and then refused to pray, wept and wailed and then turned inward and shut down. It was ugly, messy, dark, and terrifying. I wondered if I'd ever sing or smile again, or if the sun would once again shine in my heart. Prayers for wisdom gave way to prayers for my life of suffering to finally come to an end.

Then, one day, the light started to shine. Like the first green shoots pushing through the last of winter's snow, hope started to grow. I still didn't have any answers or explanations as to the reason for my suffering, but I started to see how God was using it to deliver hope and new life to others in their own seasons of despair. And as I continued to scour the worn pages of my Bible, verses I had never comprehended started to shine with understanding and insight. I could see God's wisdom and sovereignty in all things, and I was amazed at the ways He was showing me Himself. I still didn't understand Him, but that no longer mattered as much as it once had.

Why? Because I discovered I needed *Him* more than I needed to understand Him. I needed His presence more than His explanations and soul healing more than physical healing. His persistence in pursuing me, even as I wrestled with Him, overwhelmed me. What a God! Could I rest in His relentless presence even while I mourned my losses?

I'm now just months away from turning fifty. Some would say I am still a young woman with decades of life ahead. But an old soul sits in this fifty-year-old body, one that has seen and endured too much to put stock in fairy tales and unpredictable tomorrows.

Instead, I have today and the one who holds today firmly in His hands. I no longer trust my ability to control the future, but I do trust Him. Suffering will come again; I know this. But I also know that I'd rather suffer in the presence of my God than live this complicated life without Him.

And like tomorrow's flowers reaching through the hard ground toward the sun, I'm reaching for Him, regardless of what comes.

And maybe, just maybe, that is the first bloom of wisdom.

—MICHELE CUSHATT

Has there been a time in your life when suffering has drawn you closer to God? What were the circumstances and what did you learn?

_____

_____

_____

_____

Read all of Psalm 42. How does this psalm of lament give you comfort and hope even in the midst of difficult times?

_____

_____

_____

_____

In response to reading Psalm 42, write your own short psalm, poem, or prayer of how you have seen God come through for you.

_____

_____

_____

_____

SCRIPTURE MEMORY MOMENT

This week's memory verses are James 1:2–4. Write the passage in your journal or on an index card (from the NIV as printed here or from your favorite translation). Throughout the week, commit these words to memory as you ask God to create in you a heart of wisdom during times of struggle.

Consider it pure joy, my brothers and sisters, whenever you face trials of many kinds, because you know that the testing of your faith produces perseverance. Let perseverance finish its work so that you may be mature and complete, not lacking anything.

A PRAYER FOR TODAY

GOD, *thank You that my struggles aren't for naught. Thank You for being with me and being in control, even when I can't see You answering my prayers. When I feel hopeless and angry, fearful and doubtful, help me. Comfort me. Guide me with Your kindness and wisdom. Amen.*

The fear of the LORD is the beginning of wisdom,
and knowledge of the Holy One is understanding.

Proverbs 9:10

How have you become wiser through difficult circumstances?

_____

_____

_____

_____

We can't escape the possibility of hard things happening to us. When suffering doesn't relent, as Michele wrote about yesterday, it can feel ruthless and impossible to survive. I can't tell you why these things happen or how God could allow it. Life is difficult to understand, and Scripture isn't an instruction manual where we can find all the answers. As much as we all want explanations for things that don't make sense and clear directions for exactly what we need to do to make the pain stop, sometimes there simply aren't any answers. Perhaps one day we'll get to ask God about them over a cup of forever-hot coffee, but for now we may have more questions than answers. And that's a part of our faith—not a lack of it.

Wisdom gained through suffering comes from wrestling with our faith in the middle of the pain. Everything we believe gets tested in the fire of adversity. It's easy to passionately sing praise songs about how we can trust God to lead us anywhere when we're standing in the pews of our comfortable churches. But when jobs don't pan out and our marriages fall apart and depression sinks our minds into the miry muck day after day, the songs we sing and the truths we profess either become a lifeline or they prove not to be true at all. And trusting God looks less like sailing on a boat in serene waters in the middle of the ocean and more like desperately looking for a buoy while nearly drowning.

Wisdom, then, is like a scar we bear afterward—a mark, an indication that we've learned to see God in the fire and that our faith now has a tangible depth we didn't know before.

We often try to hide our scars out of shame or embarrassment, but they tell stories of what we've been through. Choose one scar you have— what story of God's faithfulness does it tell?

Read John 20:24–29. Jesus, even in His resurrected body, still had scars. When He showed them to Thomas, how did it help Thomas to believe?

When I'm in the thick of despair, I often think about how disorienting it must have been for Jesus's disciples after He died. They listened to Jesus and followed Him everywhere for three years, knowing Him intimately while not quite understanding Him (Mark 9:5–10; Luke 22:24–34; John 14:9), and now their beloved Teacher was dead. He had been nailed, pierced, and buried in a tomb. *How could it be?* they might have wondered. What were they supposed to do now? And what about everything they had been taught by Jesus and had believed in? Was any of it true anymore?

I find comfort in their despondency because even those who were once closest to Jesus were people of little faith and needed help believing. And Jesus didn't condemn them for it. Instead, He met their disbelief with His presence and power.

When a storm threatened to capsize their boat, Jesus woke up from His nap and calmed the wind and the waves. When a hungry crowd needed to be fed and the disciples had nothing to offer, Jesus multiplied bread and fed them all with plenty left over—and He did this twice (Mark 6:30–44; 8:1–13). When Thomas, who missed out on Jesus's first appearance to the disciples after the resurrection, doubted the other disciples' testimony, Jesus appeared in the room where they were gathered (John 20:24–29). These are just a few examples, and each time He loved them through their despair, disbelief, and doubts.

God has done the same for me. I can attest to His presence and power helping me believe when I couldn't muster the energy or faith. During a season of barely surviving each day while constantly grieving—the unexpected end of lifelong dreams, the deaths of loved ones, and the undercurrent of anxiety and depression—He sustained me. He gave specific words of encouragement through friends and through the random prayers of faraway acquaintances. He reminded me I wasn't alone through a coffee gift card from one of my mentees. He provided breakthroughs in my mental health and my marriage in the form of therapy and miracles.

Our struggles aren't scary for God. He isn't appalled by our doubts. He actually gives us faith in those moments when we're barely hanging on by a thread.

Our struggles aren't scary for God. He isn't appalled by our doubts. He actually *gives* us faith in those moments when we're barely hanging on by a thread. Wisdom is knowing that God is still God even when we struggle, run away, hide, and even deny Him (as Peter did in Luke 22:54–62). God's love doesn't waver, His faithfulness stays true, and His presence is the power we need to make it through anything.

What a God we have!

Read the verse for today (Prov. 9:10). How do hardships help us see God rightly? How does that lead to wisdom?

_____

_____

_____

_____

The phrase "fear of the LORD" from Proverbs 9:10 can feel convoluted. It may bring up images of a scary God we should be afraid of because of His might and holiness. Or perhaps it leads us to think we should have a healthy sense of fear for Him out of respect and honor (and also because He could zap us in righteous anger). These ideas are often affirmed by the kind of parents we had, the type of church environment we grew up in or currently attend, and the view of God preached and taught from the pulpit and in the books and media we consume.

But having a fear of the Lord is having a correct view of who God is and being in awe of Him because of who He is. Yes, He is holy and powerful, but He is also loving, kind, gentle, humble, gracious, and able to provide everything we need. He doesn't use His holiness and power against us, and one quality or character of His can't outdo or cancel out the others. The more we know Him and understand His heart for us, the more we will be able to see His magnificence and goodness.

When we have a clear view of God and trust that He is who He says He is, our perspective begins to shift. We see things with clarity—our situations, ourselves, our limitations, and even our blessings. Our circumstances may stay the same, but when our faces are turned toward His face and our eyes are brightened by His light, we see that He is all we need.

He is *everything* we need.

> Read John 14:1–11. When Philip tells Jesus that seeing the Father would be enough, how does Jesus prove that *He* is enough?

SCRIPTURE MEMORY MOMENT

Write out James 1:2–4. What trial are you facing today where you need God's wisdom and the power of His presence?

A PRAYER FOR TODAY

GOD, *thank You for being everything I need. Thank You that my doubts and struggles are not an obstacle for Your love and grace. Instead, when I can't hold on any longer because my hands are weak and I've been emptied, Your presence is with me and Your power gives me strength to carry on. When the pain of my circumstances blurs my vision, help me see You as You are. Let that be the beginning of wisdom for me. Amen.*

But whatever were gains to me I now consider loss for the sake of Christ. What is more, I consider everything a loss because of the surpassing worth of knowing Christ Jesus my Lord, for whose sake I have lost all things. I consider them garbage, that I may gain Christ and be found in him.

Philippians 3:7–9a

How have you experienced the "surpassing worth of knowing Christ Jesus my Lord" in difficult circumstances? If you haven't, what do you think it means to experience this?

Suffering has the ability to bring clarity and perspective. Things we may have considered of utmost importance no longer pull our attention. What used to be urgent and necessary becomes a wish for the future or loses its appeal completely. Pain can shrink our world into the smallest circle around us and focus our primary purpose on making it to the next day. It pauses life and helps us evaluate our priorities and relationships. Whether we're facing a tragedy, chronic pain, or the bruise of broken friendships, the palpable ache can make our desires, our beliefs, and our hope clearer.

So when the divide between us and our friends is too vast to heal, what do we have left? When we lose our financial means to maintain the life we've had, what do we do? What can we hope for when our children leave our homes or the faith we raised them in? Who do we have when our spouse neglects us or leaves us for someone else? When we experience gaslighting or abuse in the church, what do we have left to believe in?

All we have left is Jesus.

Jesus understood anguish. In Luke 22:39–46, He prays, "Father, if you are willing, take this cup from me" (v. 42). Can you hear the agony in those words? Jesus was asking the Father if there was another possible way besides the one He was about to face—death on the cross. Even after He adds "yet not my will, but yours be done," verse 44 tells us that He was still in anguish—so much so that His sweat was like drops of blood. Jesus knew the inner turmoil of facing death, with none of His closest disciples to stay awake with Him in His anguish. He understood that deep loneliness and fear.

Jesus also knew betrayal. In the events that unfolded after that prayer, Jesus was betrayed twice—once by Judas Iscariot, who sold Him out and got Him arrested, and once by Peter, who denied that he even knew Jesus (Luke 22:47–62). He understood how it felt to have close friends—people who had shared meals with Him and who had confessed loyalty and love—leave Him at the worst time of His life.

Jesus was familiar with being misunderstood—by His family (Mark 3:20–21), by His disciples (John 6:60–66), and by the crowds of people who followed Him (12:12–16). He knew what it felt like to not meet the expectations of those around Him and to be on the fringes of what others considered "normal." People often didn't understand what He was talking about or who He really was.

And in the end, Jesus knew all He had was the Father. In His anguished prayer in Luke 22 and His farewell prayer recorded in John 17, you can hear the intimacy and love He has for the Father. He knew what His purpose was, why He needed to do it, and who awaited Him at the end of it all: God the Father.

If Jesus is all we have left, then we have a God who understands loss, pain, and incredible suffering. We have a God who knows us and doesn't judge us for our worst moments or seasons of life. We have a God who stays with us when no else does, who weeps with us, and who remains present (and awake) to our troubles.

Read Hebrews 4:14–16. A high priest served as a mediator between people and God. Chosen as a representative, a high priest would sacrifice animals to atone for the sins of the people. Knowing this, what does it mean to you that Jesus is our High Priest who not only atoned for our sins by sacrificing Himself but who also sympathizes with us?

Look up Hebrews 12:1–3. How do we not lose heart in the midst of hardships?

As the perfect mediator between us and God, Jesus was the ultimate sacrifice—holy God and fully human. He was the fulfiller of prophecies and promises, and He is the hope of our lives. When we don't know how we'll make it through, we look to the one who gets it—Jesus.

In Philippians 3:10–11, Paul writes that he wants to know Christ, both in the power of His resurrection and in His sufferings. Though we can know God through other means, there is another level of knowing Him that we gain through suffering.

We shouldn't be masochists who take pleasure in life's pains. But when we do suffer, wisdom teaches us to keep our eyes open and search for God, knowing that He can be found.

In Proverbs 8:17, wisdom says, "I love those who love me, and those who seek me find me." And in Jeremiah 29:12–14, God echoes similar words to the Israelites when they are in exile: "Then you will call on me and come and pray to me, and I will listen to you. You will seek me and find me when you seek me with all your heart. I will be found by you . . . and will bring you back from captivity."

Wisdom is gained in suffering when we turn our eyes to look for God in our circumstances—even when we can't seem to see Him or hear Him. God can still be found in the silence and the void.

In our desperation for help and answers, we look for signs that prove God is really out there and aware of our pain. But consider seeing it differently: God's silence isn't His ignoring us but His coming near to us, sitting with us, and grieving as we grieve.

Perhaps you've experienced the double portion of pain when people try to comfort you with spiritual platitudes that only rub salt in the wounds. You wish for their presence instead of their fumbling,

God can still be found in the silence and the void.

unintentionally hurtful words. You'd rather have them simply be with you instead of trying to lift your spirits. Now imagine that's what God does for us. His silence doesn't mean distance, nor does a lack of signs mean neglect.

God hears us when we whisper for help through our tears and when we scream anguish from our gut. He draws near when no one else can understand, and He can be found.

When we seek Him, we will find Him and get to know Him more deeply and see the truth that Paul writes about: we gain even when we lose, because in our loss we gain Christ.

Look up Philippians 1:20–24. How do we gain Christ in life or death?

_____

_____

_____

_____

SCRIPTURE MEMORY MOMENT

Read and write out James 1:2–4 three times. As you do, consider how we need to persevere through our trials in order to mature in faith.

A PRAYER FOR TODAY

LORD, *thank You that when I seek You I will find You. When I'm in relentless pain, all I want is relief, but teach me to listen to Your wisdom so I can know Christ more. Direct my heart and my eyes to look for You. And as I experience who You are more deeply in my suffering, may that lead to wisdom in how I live my life even after the suffering passes. Amen.*

Give praise to the Lord, proclaim his name;
    make known among the nations what he has done.
Sing to him, sing praise to him;
    tell of all his wonderful acts.
Glory in his holy name;
    let the hearts of those who seek the Lord rejoice.
Look to the Lord and his strength;
    seek his face always.

Psalm 105:1–4

How does the wisdom you gain through difficult circumstances help you when the next hard thing happens?

In Michele's story this week, her unbearable suffering helped her see that she needed God more than she needed to understand Him or her suffering. Michele learned to trust Him so much that she'd rather suffer with God than be without Him. This wisdom will carry her no matter what she faces in the future.

Each time we persevere through pain and learn to find God in it, we gain not only wisdom but also a tangible moment to remember and refer back to again and again—evidence that God is who He says He is, that His promises are secure, and that His love for us is profound.

However, in order to build a history of God's faithfulness to us, we need to seek wisdom while we're in the thick of suffering, holding on to Christ until we get to the end. Maturity and wisdom aren't magically bestowed on anyone who suffers; they're learned and gained when we trust God to help us persevere.

As our Scripture memory verse for this week says, "Consider it pure joy, my brothers and sisters, whenever you face trials of many kinds, because you know that the testing of your faith produces perseverance. Let perseverance finish its work so that you may be mature and complete, not lacking anything" (James 1:2–4).

James writes that "the testing of your faith produces perseverance," meaning perseverance is a by-product of faith, not something we muster by our will and with our strength. It's all from God. God does the persevering for us; we don't persevere for Him. And as we let perseverance do its work within us, we mature in wisdom.

Isn't that freeing? How many times have we been in the middle of a struggle with no help in sight or no energy to do anything, let alone try harder in our faith? In our exhaustion, we don't need to buck up and white-knuckle our way through. Instead, we release our tight grip and let perseverance do its work. Then we continue on, persisting with patience.

> **Read James 5:7–11. How does the analogy of the farmer help you envision patience in persevering? What is implied in the farmer's posture as he waits for the autumn and spring rains?**

_____

_____

Look up Romans 12:12. How does each of these short instructions guide us as we persist with patience?

_____

_____

_____

_____

Perhaps the hardest truths to accept about suffering are that (1) life guarantees it and (2) we can't control it. We can't control when or how it happens, and we can't make it go any faster when we're in the long middle of it. Unlike movies, where resolution comes once the protagonist learns their lesson, our lives aren't so tidy and wisdom isn't so formulaic.

This is where patience comes in. Patience doesn't necessarily mean we wait with enlightened calmness, although I'm sure we would all love that. Patience is accepting the reality of our situation and bearing it—because we must and because we can't rush struggle or tragedy or grief. We can't hurry wisdom.

So we endure. We trust. We wait. Psalm 37:7 encourages us,

> Be still before the Lord
>   and wait patiently for him;
> do not fret when people succeed in their ways,
>   when they carry out their wicked schemes.

> **Lord, what do You want me to see of You? What are You doing in me that I need to be aware of?**

Being still and not fretting indicate that we let go of what might happen or what other people will do. We trust that God is working on our behalf in some way, and we seek Him in the process. We pray, *Lord, what do You want me to see of You? What are You doing in me that I need to be aware of? Holy Spirit, show me, teach me.*

Let's patiently press on in wisdom and with hope that God is working on our behalf and that one day things will shift. Because as we read in James 5:11, "The Lord is full of compassion and mercy."

> **Look up Romans 5:3–5 in the NIV and fill in the blanks.**
>
> Suffering → _____
>
> Perseverance → _____
>
> Character → _____
>
> **What does verse 5 promise?**
>
> _____
>
> _____
>
> _____
>
> _____

In the midst of suffering, hope may seem naive, as if only foolish people who can't see reality have hope. But the opposite is true. To hope is to see with spiritual eyes—with the insights of the Holy Spirit, who guides us into all truth (John 16:13). That's why hope doesn't shame or disappoint us. Our hope isn't based on lofty ideas. Our hope is founded in Christ, who broke all barriers to love us. No matter what happens in our lives, that reality doesn't change: He loves us and His love perseveres (1 Cor. 13:7).

However, even though God's love is the whole message of the gospel, of all Scripture, it's easy for us to forget. That leads us into our final thought for today: *wisdom comes from remembering.*

Our passage for today from Psalm 105:1–4 recounts God's deliverance of the Israelites from Egypt. Throughout the Bible, this story, along with many others, is often repeated to recall God's power and faithfulness and great love for His people. This is how we build a history of God's faithfulness—by writing it down, telling it to ourselves and others, and remembering. If not, we *will* forget.

After Moses delivers the greatest commandment to love the Lord, he emphasizes how important it is to remember:

> These commandments that I give you today are to be on your hearts. Impress them on your children. Talk about them when you sit at home and when you walk along the road, when you lie down and when you get up. Tie them as symbols on your hands and bind them on your foreheads. Write them on the doorframes of your houses and on your gates. (Deut. 6:6–9)

In other words, do whatever you can to remember. Write it down in your journal. Tape a note on your mirror so you can see it every day. Make it your phone lock screen. Get it tattooed on your arm.

Take some time to remember. How has God shown Himself to you in your pain or grief, in loss and suffering? How has He provided for you? Healed you? Guided you out of an unhealthy relationship? Has He proved Himself to be everything to you? Look back and see how you've become wiser and more mature through hardships, and thank God.

Draw a simple time line. From as early as you can remember, mark the date and tangible moments when you experienced God helping you persevere through difficult times.

SCRIPTURE MEMORY MOMENT

Write out James 1:2–4. As you do, ask the Lord to help you persist in patience through the tough circumstances you're in. If that's not you right now, then pray for someone else who needs God's perseverance.

A PRAYER FOR TODAY

GOD, *I'm so grateful that I don't need to rely on my own strength to persevere through difficult times. Even though I hate suffering, help me accept that hardship is a part of life and that it's not because I deserve to suffer—or worse, that You want me to suffer. Let perseverance do its work in me, and please give me patience as I keep going. Help me to trust in You. Amen.*

Praise be to the God and Father of our Lord Jesus Christ, the
Father of compassion and the God of all comfort, who comforts us in all our troubles, so that we can comfort those in
any trouble with the comfort we ourselves receive from God.

2 Corinthians 1:3–4

**How have you been comforted in your hardships by those who have gone
through similar pains? Or how have you been able to comfort others with
the wisdom you've gained through difficult circumstances?**

Strangely, like a bonfire we can all gather around, struggle brings
people together. We huddle closely, drawn to one another by our
shared pain, and find the silence a welcome reprieve. Knowing we're
not the only ones trying to survive and deal with fear and anxiety comforts us.

Though we wish we didn't have to suffer at all, finding others who are
in the same boat is a gift. There's a greater potential to be understood

and not have to explain the details of our struggles. Further, when we suffer alongside others who know God, we're brought together at the foot of the cross, and we can pour out our anguish to the one who knows it all.

Our Scripture passage for today points to God as "the Father of compassion and the God of all comfort, who comforts us in all our troubles." He is compassionate toward us in our struggles, and He comforts us when we are *in* them. He doesn't need us to rush through trials or slap on a smile while we suffer. Jesus lived on earth and understands the range of suffering that can come with it, including death, so His comfort is true consolation.

Just as we love others because God first loved us (1 John 4:19), so also we can comfort others because He first comforted us. He shows us how by the way He chose to enter into our world and live among us. Jesus cried, spoke words of hope, forgiveness, and encouragement, and met people where they were—on the streets, hiding in trees, in the dark of night, and in the middle of His own grief.

He's a God who shows up.

Read Daniel 3:8–27. In this story, what do you learn about the way God shows up?

Read John 11:17–44. Knowing He is about to face His own death, how does Jesus comfort Mary and Martha?

_____

_____

_____

_____

The comfort we give to others requires wisdom. In general, we can follow Jesus's example of showing up, offering words of encouragement, and staying with others in their pain. However, as with every other thing in life, wisdom requires us to be nuanced. What one friend might need in a crisis is not the way another friend wants you to show up. In some situations, comfort might look like writing a card because space is appreciated, and in other situations comfort might look like providing dinner because food is love. Also, what we say and how we say it can make the difference between comfort and further isolation and hurt.

Thus, we go back to wisdom's words to us in Proverbs 8. In verse 14, she says, "Counsel and sound judgment are mine; I have insight, I have power." We seek wisdom by asking the Holy Spirit, "What should I say right now? What does my friend need? How can I show up?"

The Holy Spirit may answer with a nudge in our spirit to offer our story of pain, to reach out and give a hug, or to simply offer up a prayer on a friend's behalf. We might sense that the right, Spirit-led thing to do is to be outraged alongside a friend or to agree that life just isn't fair. Perhaps what we need to do is more difficult, such as gently telling a friend the hard truth about their character or their choices in the moment. Whatever the Spirit is prompting us to do, we need to make sure that we do it out of love for the other person, not out of fear (even fear for their soul), condemnation, judgment, or our own self-righteousness. The last thing people need in the middle of hardship and pain is for us to give them unsolicited advice or spiritual admonition that's not from God.

Let's be wiser than that. Let's remember the kind of comfort that we received from God. How did He show up when we felt we couldn't handle another crisis? What words of encouragement did He have for us when we made a mistake and got ourselves into a worse situation than we'd been in? What comfort did we receive through others because of the wisdom they possessed? Take what you received and give the same to others.

> **Look up Proverbs 15:23. How have you experienced the timeliness of someone's word in your life?**

_____

_____

_____

_____

The sense of community and connection we can have with others in our mutual hardships creates solidarity, nurtures empathy, and gives us hope. I recently heard about The Human Library, where instead of checking out a book, a reader can "loan" a real person, sit down with them, and learn. The goal is to "build a positive framework for

The last thing people need in the middle of hardship and pain is for us to give them unsolicited advice or spiritual admonition that's not from God.

conversations that can challenge stereotypes and prejudices through dialogue."[1] What a fascinating and hopeful concept for people to listen and share in each other's humanity!

When we wisely and tenderly care for others in their pain, they are seen for who they are, met where they are, and given hope that they're not alone.

And we truly are not alone in our suffering.

Not only do we have each other, but we also have a history of others who have gone before us. Hebrews 12:1 says, "Therefore, since we are surrounded by such a great cloud of witnesses, let us throw off everything that hinders and the sin that so easily entangles. And let us run with perseverance the race marked out for us."

Imagine with me: You and I are running on a track with Jesus right alongside us and the power of the Holy Spirit within us. The stands are packed with faces—some familiar and some not—of people who are cheering us on. They've been on the track before. They've fallen and hurt themselves and wanted to quit in their races. They've experienced the thrill of running in their lanes and passing the baton to those who came after them. They're invested in our race and holler our names and shout encouragement: "You can do it!"

They are the cloud of witnesses—a whole spiritual heritage of witnesses, including our own ancestors who have walked the path before us.

Do you see it? We are not alone. Through shared stories of struggle and testimonies of how God empowered us to persevere, strengthened us, and wept with us, we comfort and reflect hope to one another—hope for the present, difficult moment and hope for the kingdom to come.

It's easy to believe we're the only one experiencing hardship when we're going through it. So let's end this week remembering those who have come alongside us and those whom we can come alongside. Write down their names and text them a note of thanks or encouragement.

SCRIPTURE MEMORY MOMENT

Test yourself on James 1:2–4. Try to say it out loud or write it from memory. As we move into the next week of our study, continue to reflect on these words.

A PRAYER FOR TODAY

LORD, *thank You for comforting me in my troubles and for being a God who understands. Teach me to comfort and show up for others as You have done for me, and I ask for wisdom in knowing how to do that with love and gentleness. Thank You that I'm not alone, no matter what I'm going through, because You are with me. Amen.*

WISDOM IS LEARNED THROUGH COMMUNITY

Each week so far, we've discussed how wisdom is learned, not bestowed, which means that we have to be intentional about choosing wisdom. In week 1, we learned that we gain wisdom by understanding knowledge and not just amassing it. Week 2 taught us that we learn to be wise by listening to the Holy Spirit and walking in obedience. Week 3 showed us that we can grow in wisdom as we persevere through trying circumstances. And this week, we'll explore how wisdom is learned through community.

The genius behind God's design for us to be in community is that we constantly have opportunities to hear God's voice, learn from others, and live by wisdom. Though we're imperfect, the design of community is perfect to make us more like Christ.

As you read our opening story from (in)courage writer Mary Carver, think about how learning in community with others is a path to wisdom.

A Story of Learning Wisdom

My phone was blowing up again. The text thread with two of my closest friends was calling my name and begging for a response. As I scrolled through the string of messages, I sighed in frustration. *What was I supposed to say?*

Both of these friends had experienced some serious trauma over the past few years. My own life hadn't been without challenges either, and

I was grateful they were willing to walk through hard seasons together. Though we'd met when life seemed simpler, our friendship had stood the test of many difficulties as we linked arms and offered one another support and encouragement whenever it was needed.

But when one of my friends faced a particularly sticky situation—something I'd never gone through myself and was ill-equipped to even address—I felt helpless. I knew what I wanted to say, but I wasn't sure my instincts were right this time. Normally, my tendency to rage with righteous anger on behalf of an injured friend and my penchant for fiery pep talks were, if not called for, at least somewhat beneficial. Normally, I felt confident in offering advice for whatever a friend was going through. This time, though, I was out of my depth. I worried that stoking my friend's fire with anger, encouragement, or a suggested solution to her problem might actually hurt more than help. Something held me back from responding right away.

It was time for me to sit on my hands (literally, as they were itching to text a reply to my hurting friend) and allow someone else to lead. Though our third friend was nearly a decade younger than me, I recognized that her unique background gave her insight and understanding that I simply did not have this time. Sure enough, my young friend replied to all, sharing her own experience and what she'd learned through it. She calmly advised our overwhelmed friend, giving her straightforward action steps to take as she addressed her problem.

"Yes, what she said!" I then texted. "And I love you! You can do this. God is with you!"

Again, I sighed, this time in relief. The advice our young friend gave was nearly the opposite of the response I'd initially typed out, yet I immediately knew she was right. Waiting for someone wiser than me to lead the way had been the right thing to do.

That text conversation may seem like a small moment, but it was big for me. Realizing and accepting that I might not always have the right answer was eye-opening—and difficult. Because I had experienced a variety of hard situations over the years, I'd started to believe that I could have an answer for anything a friend might face. I've prided myself on being someone who takes care of her people and have relished the role of "mom" in several friend groups. But as it turns out, I don't know everything, and some situations are way beyond my ability to fix.

For most of my adult life I've leaned heavily on a lesson my mom taught me as a child. Anytime we encountered a less-than-friendly customer service employee, she would smile big and speak with her most cheerful voice. Once we left the store or the drive-through, she'd remind me that we didn't know what that person was dealing with. She taught me to use my imagination and think outside myself, giving people the benefit of the doubt while also working to understand their different perspectives or experiences.

That approach has served me well, from allowing me to remain calm when cashiers are grouchy to helping me listen to friends of color explain their lived experiences that are vastly different from anything I've gone through or can fully grasp. Imagining what other people might be going through was a muscle I grew as I listened to and read stories by and about people dealing with issues I had never faced, like divorce or abuse or racism or adoption. Even learning about people who live in other parts of the world or past eras of history confirmed that while humanity shares many universal experiences and feelings, I definitely didn't know what it was like to live a life different from mine.

And yet, for years I still tried to fulfill the responsibility I had given myself to have an answer for every friend in every situation. After all, I *had* seen some things! And imagining what someone else was going through had given me empathy even when I didn't understand the nuances of a friend's life. But as it turns out, it's not always my job or my place to speak into a person's problem. In some situations, I don't know the solution, and that's when it's time for me to sit back and let someone else share their wisdom. Then, if it's truly beneficial, I can offer my own gifts.

Giving space to my friend to step in was hard for me, but I was so glad I'd felt prompted to do so that day. As I reflected on how that conversation played out, I was grateful to see how God reminded me to be quick to listen and slow to speak. I'm thankful He humbled me and allowed me to see how much wisdom others have—teaching me in turn to be a little wiser when it's my turn to help.

—MARY CARVER

Who has been an unlikely source of wisdom in your life?

Look up Proverbs 27:17. What does this verse tell you about the need for community in gaining wisdom?

Read Proverbs 19:20. What are the two imperatives in this proverb that teach us how we become wise?

SCRIPTURE MEMORY MOMENT

This week's memory verse is James 3:13. Write the verse in your journal or on an index card (from the NIV as printed here or from your favorite translation). Throughout the week, commit these words to memory as you ask God to create in you a heart of wisdom during times of waiting.

Who is wise and understanding among you? Let them show it by their good life, by deeds done in the humility that comes from wisdom.

A PRAYER FOR TODAY

GOD, *thank You for designing us to need each other in community. It can be painful to be sharpened by another's wisdom, but remind me in those moments that I am becoming more like Jesus through the work of the Holy Spirit. Keep me humble and pliable, ready to learn and receive wisdom from others. In doing so, make me wiser. Amen.*

But in fact God has placed the parts in the body, every one of
them, just as he wanted them to be. If they were all one part,
where would the body be? As it is, there are many parts, but
one body.

1 Corinthians 12:18–20

What are some benefits of being part of a community, whether part of a church or outside of it?

_____

_____

_____

_____

As a child, the ocean fascinated me with its unending mystery, yet it
terrified me for the same reason. Its creatures often seemed to border
on the mythical and mystical, like seahorses, narwhals, and dolphins.
At one point in time, I believed I'd grow up to be a marine biologist or
work at SeaWorld so I could spend my days studying animals—and perhaps teach them to do tricks.

I clearly had no idea what marine biologists do, but what has stayed
with me all these years is the vastness of the ocean and how there is

still so much we don't know about it. According to the National Ocean Service, "Scientists estimate that 91 percent of ocean species have yet to be classified, and that more than 80 percent of our ocean is unmapped, unobserved, and unexplored."[1]

The ocean is a mystery—not to be conquered or controlled but to inspire awe and teach us more.

Community in its broadest sense, and particularly the body of Christ, can be seen in a similar way. There is so much beauty and depth and wisdom we don't yet know about. But we can learn if we're willing, curious, and courageous to step out of the box we're in.

For many of us who grew up in the North American Christian church and who have lived most of our lives in the United States, it might be difficult to imagine anything beyond what we've been taught about our faith from the churches we grew up in, the youth group leaders we learned from, and the Christian books we were told were foundational. For some of us, it might even feel wrong to explore outside of our traditional beliefs because learning outside the box feels like a slippery slope to disbelief.

But what if we considered "out of the box" not as something dangerous but as a place where God is too? What if we opened our minds and hearts to learn from others because the Holy Spirit lives in them too? How much more might we see the vastness and wonder and power of God if we did?

Read 1 Corinthians 12:14–20. What does this passage tell you about why we need each other?

Think about the diverseness of gifts and the diversity[2] of humankind. How does that reflect who God is?

_____

_____

_____

_____

No matter how much we study and try to figure out who God is, there is still more to discover, know, and be delighted by. The vastness of humanity, of the ocean, and of all creation is a glimpse of who God is, and even those examples can't fully encompass the magnitude of God.

This is why God placed us in communities: so we can experience glimpses of His divineness in our everyday life. While we need one another to be made more like Christ (we'll talk about this on day 4), we also need one another to see more of God—His character, glory, power, joy, and wisdom.

In this way, our limitedness is a benefit to us, not a weakness. It helps us see that we _must_ depend on one another to experience God more fully. It reveals that we have access to knowledge, insight, and Holy Spirit discernment through one another. Wisdom, then, is understanding what God has provided and actively seeking Him through what He's made available to us—namely, the diverseness of the body of Christ within the communities where He has placed us.

As I shared at the beginning of this Bible study, I grew up in a church where a particular theology was highly prioritized above all others. The emphasis on its being the most biblical interpretation of Scripture left no room for the possibility that there were other ways of understanding God and His truths.

> Our limitedness is a benefit to us, not a weakness. It helps us see that we **must** depend on one another to experience God more fully.

I scoffed at the idea that theologies and theologians from other parts of the world could be just as valid or trustworthy as the ones I had been raised on. But God began to pry open my closed mind to the intentional diverseness of the body of Christ that *He* has orchestrated—diverse in race, culture, and perspectives of theology. My narrow-mindedness had led to a narrow view of God, but in His mercy, He kept blowing Himself out of every box I tried to place Him in, showing me that He would not be bound by whatever finite ideas I or any other person had of Him.

Even now, the more I come to know God, the bigger He seems to get.

Wisdom has taught me to constantly reevaluate how I see God by widening the scope of books I read, pastors and leaders I listen to, theological perspectives I learn from, and friends I seek out. Not only that, but the wisdom I've gained is more nuanced, more insightful, and deeper in value as I see more of God through others.

Consider how you learn about God—what you read and listen to, who you surround yourself with, who you trust as teachers and preachers of God's Word. Do they reflect the diverseness God desires us to learn from in the body of Christ? If not, what is one way you can begin to broaden your view of God?

_____

_____

_____

In 1 Corinthians 12:17, the visual of the whole body being an eye is a comical yet effective analogy of what it would be like to only learn and gain wisdom from people with the same perspective or background. That's not how God intended it to be.

We need people who can hear from the Holy Spirit in ways we might not. We need brothers and sisters from different backgrounds, cultures, and socioeconomic statuses to teach us from their perspective. We need artists to show us God through paint strokes and creative lettering so we can see Him just as we would through a Bible study like this one. We need praise songs from the global church to expand our ideas of what worship is supposed to look like. As our passage for today says, "If they were all one part, where would the body be?" (1 Cor. 12:19).

Thus, the wisdom we can gain is twofold: the wisdom of learning from people whose perspectives are different from our own, and the wisdom we gain from them in how to see God.

Let's choose to be wise, accepting our limitedness as an invitation to learn from others. And let's praise God for the beauty of needing one another, a design that keeps us humble and draws us closer to Him.

Read Paul's doxology in Romans 11:33–36. Write your own prayer of praise for who God is in His vastness and depth.

SCRIPTURE MEMORY MOMENT

Write out James 3:13. In what area of your life is God teaching you to be humble and learn from others?

A PRAYER FOR TODAY

LORD, *You were wise to create us to need one another. Thank You for showing me today that it's for my own benefit to be part of a body and not be on my own. Keep me humble and willing to learn from the diverseness You provide through the communities I'm in. I want to know You more! Amen.*

DAY 3

Plans fail for lack of counsel,
but with many advisers they succeed.
Proverbs 15:22

Who is a part of your community (however you might choose to define that)?

_____

_____

_____

_____

Yesterday we discussed how we can't see the fullness of God or experience the vastness of His beauty and wisdom apart from others. Community, therefore, is the ideal pairing to our limitedness, and wisdom encourages us to seek and find God wherever we are.

So let's begin today by defining the different kinds of community we can have. Though we can do this in various ways, for this study we'll categorize them by _place_, _practice_, and _purpose_. Some relationships may fall into more than one category, so keep in mind that these are basic generalizations. The point is to expand our understanding of where we can seek God's wisdom so we can pay attention and find it.

Place

Community formed by place is based on where we're located or wherever we find ourselves in life, whether by choice or not. First, we are a part of families with parents, caregivers, siblings, or other relatives, whether blood-related or not. Our family relationships often shape our initial and most imprinted view of God, self, and the world because of their proximity and depth and the amount of time we spend with family in our formative years. Seeing God in our family members can be the easiest or the hardest thing to do.

Second, we are a part of the neighborhoods and local communities in which we reside. From the friends we make next door or at school to the aunties and uncles we have in our parents' friends, these are people we're invested in and who invest in us, both intentionally and by proximity.

In whatever location we find ourselves, God teaches us to look for Him in the ordinary places and people where we might not expect to see Him, because He can be found.

Practice

Community formed by practice is based on what we do, such as work, or what we believe together with others, such as church. Work may not be the first place that comes to mind when you think of community, but when most of our adult life is spent with our coworkers, it naturally becomes a community we're part of. Through the conversations we have, the culture and unspoken rules we need to abide by, and the values that are affirmed or rejected, we learn wisdom we might not find elsewhere.

Church may be the most obvious place to find community because there we're brought together by our deepest beliefs. However, we know that church can also be a painful place to try building community. Though we see God through the praise songs and sermons, finding

God in one another can be fraught with disappointment. Still, God is there, waiting to be found.

God is moving in the communities where we work and worship, and through them He teaches us to discern how the Spirit is moving.

Purpose

Community formed by purpose is based on what we're interested in or passionate about. The bond we feel with this community can be intense and inspiring because we're motivated by the same thing. This could be a cause or a hobby or an art form. It could be volunteering, serving, or creating together. The purpose could be goal-oriented or task-driven. Whether or not the purpose is faith-based, God is in the midst of the work, giving visions and dreams to make the world a better place.

The wisdom we gain from these communities can remind us to keep an eternal perspective in the midst of struggles, setbacks, and lack of clarity.

God is present in all of these communities, and each one can gift us wisdom through the relationships we have in them. The question is, are we seeking God and His wisdom wherever we are?

> Reread today's passage from Proverbs 15:22. What is the benefit of being in communities, particularly ones with wise people in them?

The question is, are we seeking God and His wisdom wherever we are?

_____

_____

Look up Proverbs 12:26. Reflect on the close relationships you have within each of your communities. Whom have you chosen to be your sources of counsel, and are they wise choices?

_____

_____

_____

_____

The potential for wisdom is everywhere in our communities. Since we have the privilege of accessing it wherever we are, we must be responsible to seek it and listen to it and diligently test the counsel we receive against the wisdom of God.

Let's look at the story of Moses and Jethro in Exodus 18. Jethro, Moses's father-in-law, comes to visit him in the desert where the Israelites are camped. After catching up on what happened after Moses led the Israelites out of Egypt (crossing the Red Sea and escaping from the Egyptian army), Jethro notices how much Moses is doing for the people and advises him that what he's doing isn't good. He says to Moses,

> You and these people who come to you will only wear yourselves out. The work is too heavy for you; you cannot handle it alone. Listen now to me and I will give you some advice, and may God be with you. You must be the people's representative before God and bring their disputes to him. Teach them his decrees and instructions, and show them the way they are to live and how they are to behave. But select capable men from all the people—men who fear God, trustworthy men who hate

> dishonest gain—and appoint them as officials over thousands, hundreds, fifties and tens. Have them serve as judges for the people at all times, but have them bring every difficult case to you; the simple cases they can decide themselves. That will make your load lighter, because they will share it with you. If you do this and God so commands, you will be able to stand the strain, and all these people will go home satisfied. (vv. 18–23)

Jethro advises Moses on what he should do and then adds, "If you do this *and God so commands*." He not only shares his wisdom on how to handle the problem Moses is facing, but he also tells Moses to double-check his advice with God.

Sometimes wisdom will come to us as it did for Moses, and other times we will need to seek out trusted people for wisdom. But either way, we need to be open to hearing counsel from others and taking in what they say with a grain of salt, as we've discussed before, while not being defensive or prideful. Then we bring their advice to God. We ask in prayer whether their advice lines up with what God has been saying already or what we sense God is leading us into. We continue to seek God's counsel until we have a sense of peace or He confirms it over time in various ways. Ultimately, the wisdom we want the most is God's, and He will give it if we ask.

Let's put this into practice. Who has given you advice recently? Is this person wise and trustworthy? What was their advice? How is God confirming or not confirming it?

SCRIPTURE MEMORY MOMENT

Read and write out James 3:13 three times. Reach out to the trusted people within your communities to thank them for being a source of wisdom in your life.

A PRAYER FOR TODAY

GOD, *thank You for the communities You've placed me in. Thank You for the people in my life who have shown me how to be wise and who have guided me when I didn't know what to do or where to go: [name them specifically here]. And thank You for being the ultimate source of counsel for my life. You never lead me astray or leave me on my own. How gracious You are! Amen.*

DAY 4

For by the grace given me I say to every one of you: Do not think of yourself more highly than you ought, but rather think of yourself with sober judgment, in accordance with the faith God has distributed to each of you. For just as each of us has one body with many members, and these members do not all have the same function, so in Christ we, though many, form one body, and each member belongs to all the others.

Romans 12:3–5

How do we make sure to keep our heart soft and open to learn from others?

Our limitedness is an invitation to seek community, and within our communities we experience the sharpening and refining that happens when we learn from one another (Prov. 27:17).

Once upon a time, my husband was a chef (now he's a software engineer). Many chefs have their own knives that they take to work because they see a knife as an extension of their hands, a tool to express their craft. Every time my husband's knives became dull, he had a whole routine to get them back to their sharpest. Using a water-soaked sharpening stone laid on a kitchen towel, he would steadily and swiftly swipe the knife blade across the stone. Each swish filed down the dullness until a new layer of steel emerged to be shaped into a sharp edge.

I would watch, fascinated. Sharpening happened by deliberate movements, not by striking or pounding the metal.

We become like Christ in a similar way. The people in our various communities are sharpening stones who help grind away our selfishness and pride, our bent toward idolatry, and our tendency to think too much about ourselves. We do this for one another. It's one of the blessings of being in community, even though the process can be painful.

Sharpening can happen with our closest friends whom we've given permission to keep us accountable. It can come from sources we may not always appreciate, such as our parents, our leaders, or even our children. It can happen with anyone who crosses our path in church, at work, or online.

We need wisdom to sharpen one another with humility, grace, and love, and we also need wisdom to receive the sharpening for ourselves.

Read Proverbs 11:2 and Proverbs 12:15. Why is humility so important for gaining wisdom in and from community?

Sometimes it's helpful to consider the opposite reality of a situation in order to better understand what we're aiming for. What are some examples of sharpening one another *without* humility, grace, and love? How have you seen this play out in your communities of place, practice, and purpose?

_____

_____

_____

_____

Learning to be humble in order to be wise starts with dying to our ego and having an unobstructed view of ourselves. For our purposes, I use the word *ego* to refer to a self-importance that's synonymous with pride, not to indicate a sense of self. It should also not be confused with self-esteem or self-worth, which are completely different from having an inflated ego.

When we think of ourselves more highly than we ought, as our passage for today talks about, our ego blocks wisdom. When we're convinced that our own knowledge, insight, or help is better than that of others, we place ourselves on a pedestal no human can—or should—stand on. The way we view ourselves becomes distorted because we aren't on the same level, looking eye to eye with others who can reflect our humanness back to us. Instead of thinking with sober judgment, we begin to consider ourselves on par with God, thus becoming foolish instead of wise.

In Luke 18, Jesus tells a parable to "some who were confident of their own righteousness and looked down on everyone else" (v. 9). In the story, a Pharisee and a tax collector come to the temple to pray. The Pharisee prays a monologue about how good he is in comparison to some other people, like the tax collector. He sees his own righteousness as a means of qualifying himself before God and forgets that he should be praising God instead (vv. 10–12).

The tax collector, on the other hand, beats his chest and cries out, "God, have mercy on me, a sinner" (v. 13). He has a correct, clear view of himself as a person standing in God's presence. He knows that his lack of righteousness means he must rely on God's mercy.

Wisdom teaches us that we're no better than the next person. Not only are we all in need of God's righteousness and saving grace, but in Christ, we all have access to the Father and the Holy Spirit to teach us, infuse us with wisdom, and speak through us. Wisdom, then, is self-awareness and humility, knowing we're all in need of God's wisdom and grace and that we don't belong on a pedestal.

Only God deserves and can hold that kind of glory.

> **Read Matthew 7:1–5. What does this passage teach us about judging ourselves and others soberly?**

When we are the one sharpening another, our humility also needs to be accompanied by grace and love toward the other person.

> **Wisdom is self-awareness and humility, knowing we're all in need of God's wisdom and grace and that we don't belong on a pedestal.**

You may be familiar with the phrase "Speak the truth in love," which comes from Ephesians 4:15. It's a common sentiment used as permission to cuttingly sharpen one another with truth, whether true or not. We might think, *I can say that to her because I love her and I know she's straying away from the truth.* Or, *Truth is truth, and if she can't handle it, then that's her problem. I love her, but she needs to know.*

However, when we use that verse as a hammer to wield against others, we lack wisdom and understanding of the truth of Christ. Reading verse 15 in context shows how the outcome of speaking the truth in love is that "we will grow to become in every respect the mature body of him who is the head, that is Christ. From him the whole body, joined and held together by every supporting ligament, grows and builds itself up in love, as each part does its work" (vv. 15–16).

Love builds up. The life of Jesus from beginning to end was about love. And whatever truth we speak must point to that. It must point to Jesus, who is the truest Truth (John 14:6), and how He lived and died for us. Then we may consider if, when, and how to speak the truth with love.

Wisdom helps us to distinguish not just right from wrong but truth with love. This is sharpening done right.

SCRIPTURE MEMORY MOMENT

Write out James 3:13. As you do, choose one piece of wisdom you've learned this week and think about how you can apply it in your life.

A PRAYER FOR TODAY

LORD, *forgive me for the times when I've pounded the truth onto someone instead of sharpening them with love. Teach me another way by Your wisdom. I also pray for the humility to receive and learn wisdom from others, because the Holy Spirit is in them too. Help me to keep my ego in check and to keep my praises focused on You. Amen.*

DAY 5

After this I looked, and there before me was a great multitude
that no one could count, from every nation, tribe, people
and language, standing before the throne and before the
Lamb. They were wearing white robes and were holding palm
branches in their hands. And they cried out in a loud voice:

"Salvation belongs to our God,
who sits on the throne,
and to the Lamb."

Revelation 7:9–10

**What do you imagine heaven will be like? How does that image affect
your view of community?**

As we end this week, let's weave together a bigger picture of how being
part of a community and learning wisdom from one another gives us a
glimpse of what we read about in Revelation 21:1–4. John writes,

> Then I saw "a new heaven and a new earth," for the first heaven and the first earth had passed away, and there was no longer any sea. I saw the Holy City, the new Jerusalem, coming down out of heaven from God, prepared as a bride beautifully dressed for her husband. And I heard a loud voice from the throne saying, "Look! God's dwelling place is now among the people, and he will dwell with them. They will be his people, and God himself will be with them and be their God. 'He will wipe every tear from their eyes. There will be no more death' or mourning or crying or pain, for the old order of things has passed away."

This is what we look forward to as the full and final redemption of God's creation—a new heaven and a new earth in which any distinction or separation between the two no longer exists. In the beginning, the world was created by God—the Father, Son, and Holy Spirit (Gen. 1:26)—and from this loving community came the birth of another community: God communing with His creation, Adam and Eve. But this perfect union was broken by sin, and since then God has been working to redeem humankind to Himself and reconcile heaven and earth back together again.

The hope of this was made possible in Jesus's death on the cross because He *was* heaven on earth. And now, in Him, we are walking dwelling places of the Holy Spirit, little tabernacles of God's presence here on earth (1 Cor. 6:19). Glimpses of heaven break through when we live like Jesus in our communities, until the day when all is made right and we're once again in perfect union with God.

Read the Lord's Prayer in Matthew 6:9–13, focusing on verse 10. How is community a tangible example of "on earth as it is in heaven"?

> **Our diversity and complexity as people are meant to reflect God's uniqueness and vastness.**

If we are to be a community that reflects heaven on earth, how does that vision inform the way we ought to be in community with one another?

_____

_____

_____

_____

In His work of redemption, God continuously threads the gap that was created by sin. Weaving us together in community allows us to experience the richness and beauty of what the church is meant to be.

But in our not yet fully redeemed world, the church often looks messy and broken instead of beautiful. Our diversity and complexity as people are meant to reflect God's uniqueness and vastness, but those are the very things that can create friction, misunderstanding, and pain that do not reflect the kingdom to come. It can be discouraging and heartbreaking, and working to love one another toward maturity can feel hopeless.

If you're in the middle of that hardship, you're not there alone. Jesus understands where you are and is there with you. He's interacted with people who claim to know God but don't. He's been rejected and lonely in the midst of community. And He held the tension and weight of heaven and earth, divine and mortal, the holiness of God and the sin of all humanity in His body on the cross. He endured because He loves us, and now He sits at the right hand of God interceding for us (Rom. 8:34).

God knows we won't always get along with everyone or love them perfectly. We're all in the process of being redeemed, and unlike humans, only God can love perfectly. Still, even in our imperfections, we are called to seek wisdom and ask the Holy Spirit to keep renewing us inwardly and in our communities. We pray for the kingdom to break through on earth as it is in heaven, and we pray for that to happen in our midst.

When we fix our eyes on eternity and on the coming kingdom, letting that guide us forward, we can stand in the muck *and* have hope. We can see the brokenness in our current situations *and* still believe that change can happen. We can hold the vision of a new heaven and new earth with people from every nation, tribe, people, and language *and* work to make that vision a reality right where we're at.

We stay in community[3] and learn to "clothe" ourselves with "compassion, kindness, humility, gentleness and patience" and to "bear with each other and forgive one another," forgiving as God forgave us (Col. 3:12–13). This is God's design to make us more like Him and prepare us for the kingdom to come. May we be a community on earth as it will be in heaven.

> **Look up Revelation 21:5; Isaiah 43:19; and Isaiah 65:17. How do these verses encourage you in the tension of the already (redeemed) but not yet (fully redeemed)?**

So, what would we look like if we lived formed by the kingdom to come? Our memory verse for this week tells us:

> Who is wise and understanding among you? Let them show it by their good life, by deeds done in the humility that comes from wisdom. (James 3:13)

Our life will bear the fruit of wisdom and knowledge of God's saving truth. To show it by our life means that we exhibit a consistent pattern of faith in action in our everyday. Micah 6:8 boils it down to a simple sentence: "To act justly and to love mercy and to walk humbly with your God."

And all examples of this point back to Jesus, who embodied justice, mercy, and humility. Let's be wise and be like Him. Let's be glimpses of heaven on earth to those around us so they, too, can share the hope we have that one day all will be made new.

Write out the Lord's Prayer. You can choose the Matthew 6:9–13 version or whatever version your church uses.

SCRIPTURE MEMORY MOMENT

Test yourself on James 3:13. Try to say it out loud or write it below from memory. As we move into the next week of our study, continue to reflect on these words.

A PRAYER FOR TODAY

GOD, *thank You for the beautiful picture of what the new heaven and new earth will be like. I long to experience this more in real life! When being in community is painful, guide me through the mess. Help me to love as You do and to remember that You are in the midst of it all, making Yourself known. Renew me and Your church again and again until we see You face-to-face. Amen.*

WISDOM IS LEARNED THROUGH PRACTICE

Perhaps you've heard the phrase "Practice makes progress." Instead of the unachievable goal of perfection, we practice so that we can get better at whatever skill we're working on. We can apply the same principle to wisdom: practicing wisdom makes us wiser. It may sound redundant, but we can't grow in wisdom until we intentionally make an effort to become wise.

Just as practice is necessary for training to run a half marathon, learning to play piano, or improving our cooking skills, we take what we learn from our life experiences, the knowledge we learn about God and ourselves, and the insight we gain from the Holy Spirit and our community, and we rehearse wisdom again and again.

As you read this opening story from (in)courage writer Melissa Zaldivar, think about how practice makes progress when it comes to wisdom.

A Story of Learning Wisdom

I struggle to practice things over and over again. When I was in elementary school, I took piano lessons for one year. Each week, I had to show my piano teacher a log of all the hours I'd practiced that week. Each day had a little space where I could fill in the time, and every week in the minutes before piano lessons, I made up arbitrary numbers because the truth was I hadn't practiced much.

As I grew up, I realized that repetition is often boring but also entirely necessary. I learned to repeat the same mundane tasks. I wrote the same Hebrew words over and over again as I committed them to memory. I cleaned countless golf clubs at the course where I worked. Over time I learned that a habit is built when we commit to doing the same thing more than once.

When it comes to wisdom, we don't only have to consider or apply it one time. No, we have the chance to really build that muscle by continually turning to Jesus and asking Him what's best. When we make it a habit to draw near to Him, it eventually becomes muscle memory.

In college, I made it a point to write out rules for myself about how I wanted to live. For example, I needed to go to bed early so I wouldn't be so groggy in the morning. Or I wouldn't allow myself to make major life choices without praying about them. While that might seem obvious, writing it down motivated me to take it more seriously.

It wasn't that I wanted approval from God as if He was signing some cosmic permission slip. I wasn't running it by Him in case it needed a second set of eyes either. This rule had to do with wanting to bring Him the things that were heaviest on my heart in an act of relational trust. If I wanted to move forward with something, I wanted to move forward with Him.

Usually, I would pray through something and feel peace to make it happen. But a few times I've felt a distinct impression that I wasn't supposed to take the step I was considering. One such moment happened when I was inspired to start a project called Cheer Her On. I woke up one morning with a clear idea of what it would be: a community of women talking about discipleship. I wrote down the main values, the branding ideas, and the scriptural support, and then brainstormed some creative processes. My friends loved it, and it seemed like a God-sent idea.

But then, trying to build the muscle of trusting God's wisdom and insight, I decided to pause and listen. Two words kept coming to the surface: *not yet*. It made no sense. I had the bandwidth and the resources and the drive. It was a good, God-honoring idea. Why wouldn't this be the best time?

Years of intentionally and consistently taking things to God first had led me to this crossroads even though it didn't make a whole lot of sense. Still, I knew I needed to trust the process, so I set the project aside, and time passed until I forgot it even existed.

I moved across the country and started a new job, and before I knew it, two years had passed. One afternoon, I found myself writing a note to a friend who was moving away to a town where I'd previously lived. As I told her what restaurants to eat at and what places to visit, I felt joy in passing along what I'd learned. And that's when it came back to me: it was time for Cheer Her On.

The timing was right, but more than that, my heart was right. If I'd launched it sooner, I would have put a lot of my own identity and hope into the project. I would have looked to it for my legitimacy and burned myself out. But years later, after more counseling and personal development, it seemed to be a sweet spot more than a stumbling block.

What I want you to know is this: When I first started handing things to Jesus, I had a white-knuckle grip. I wanted to do things my way and in my own timing. But by committing to seek God's wisdom, I avoided heartache and striving. I sensed more confidence in the task at hand because I was walking in wisdom with God, not just running my ideas past Him like a supervisor.

I am learning that we don't have all the info. We don't know what's coming or what will be best. But God does. And while it sometimes makes no sense in the moment, farther along we'll see the ways He was orchestrating things all along. Wisdom isn't just knowledge; it's also timing and repetition. As we bring things to God and ask for His wisdom over and over again, it becomes our instinct. And when we make it our default to pursue His will ahead of our own, our motivations line up in a direction that points our own heart and others to who He is and what He's doing.

So put in the hard work of repeatedly handing things back to God and asking for His wisdom. Over time, it'll become second nature, and I promise it'll be worth it.

—MELISSA ZALDIVAR

Write down an example from your life where practice made progress. What were some things you learned about the process of progress?

_____

_____

_____

_____

Look up 1 Timothy 4:15 in the CSB, ESV, and NIV. Fill in the blanks below. How do these phrases deepen your understanding of what practice means?

CSB: "Practice these things; _____ ,
       so that your progress may be evident to all."

ESV: "Practice these things, _____ ,
       so that all may see your progress."

NIV: "Be diligent in these matters; _____ ,
       so that everyone may see your progress."

SCRIPTURE MEMORY MOMENT

This week's memory verses are Matthew 7:24–25. Write the passage in your journal or on an index card (from the NIV as printed here or from your favorite translation). Throughout the week, commit these words to memory and ask God to create in you a heart of wisdom as you practice what He's taught you thus far.

> *Therefore everyone who hears these words of mine and puts them into practice is like a wise man who built his house on the rock. The rain came down, the streams rose, and the winds blew and beat against that house; yet it did not fall, because it had its foundation on the rock.*

A PRAYER FOR TODAY

GOD, *thank You for the grace of learning over time and for the repeated opportunities to practice wisdom in my life. Thank You for being patient with me in the process and being willing to keep teaching me when I don't get it the first or the hundredth time. Help me not to begrudge the discipline of repetition but to receive Your instruction as a gift. Amen.*

DAY 2

Why do you call me, "Lord, Lord," and do not do what I say? As for everyone who comes to me and hears my words and puts them into practice, I will show you what they are like. They are like a man building a house, who dug down deep and laid the foundation on rock. When a flood came, the torrent struck that house but could not shake it, because it was well built. But the one who hears my words and does not put them into practice is like a man who built a house on the ground without a foundation. The moment the torrent struck that house, it collapsed and its destruction was complete.

Luke 6:46–49

Think about your home or the building where you work or attend church. Picture all that goes on inside these structures and how much they endure over the years. Why do you think it's important that they have a solid foundation?

Every functional thing has a foundation on which it's built—buildings, organizations, marriages, friendships, and faith. The foundation determines the strength and quality, the stability and durability of the object. Depending on its sturdiness, the foundation can either have the ability to hold and protect its occupants, or it can crack, crumble, and destroy lives. Building a solid foundation is essential for both survival and flourishing, and it takes intention, time, and practice.

In our passage for today, Jesus says that those who practice His words are people who dig deep and lay a foundation on rock. They have foresight for what's needed not only when the weather's balmy but also and especially when unexpected storms come in. They understand the necessity and purpose of a foundation, so they take measures to make sure they can stay grounded no matter what happens. They dig deep until they reach the rock, even though that requires effort and discipline. Even if they can't see the rewards of their labor at the moment, they know laying a foundation will benefit them in the long run.

Without the wisdom of practice, we are like the man who builds his house on the ground without a foundation. It might take less time, but when hardship comes, we lose everything and are left back at square one, needing to rebuild from the ground up.

Let's choose wisdom and not foolishness. Let's choose the mundane but necessary work of practice so we can build on a firm foundation.

> **Read Psalm 118:22; Isaiah 28:16; and Acts 4:10–12. What do you think it means that Jesus is the stone on which we build our foundation?**

The wise man laid his foundation on rock because in order for a building to withstand natural forces, the foundation must be built on something sturdy. If we choose to be wise, we lay our foundation on Jesus, who is our rock. From there, we build up. We structure our values and beliefs on what He was like, how He interacted with people, what He taught, and whom He focused on in His ministry. We learn from the kind of intimate relationship He had with God the Father and from His rhythms of life that we can infer from the gospel texts.

In the passages listed above, we read about Jesus being the capstone or cornerstone. In times past, this would have been the first stone laid when constructing a building. Though today it's only symbolic, long ago the cornerstone regulated how all the other stones were laid. The strength and durability of the entire building were determined by the cornerstone, and this is why it's so meaningful that Jesus is our rock, our foundation, our cornerstone. Everything else can shift and sink, shake and break, but He stays solid, unmoving, steady. Everything we practice, all the wisdom we can learn, starts with Him and stems from Him.

> **Read Colossians 1:16–18 two times. Write down all the ways Christ is supreme above all else.**

When we make it a habit—a practice—to be and live like Jesus, we can stand on a solid foundation of faith. These habits are formed in ordinary, mundane seasons through repetition and daily practice. By building muscle memories of trust and faithful obedience, we can withstand the trials that test our faith when they come.

When I was growing up overseas as a missionary kid, I spent more hours practicing piano than I did being homeschooled. If school took up three hours of my day, I spent six hours running my fingers along the black and white keys, practicing my scales and sonatas. The hope was that by the time recitals came around, my body and mind would be so familiar with the notes that I'd be able to play from memory, almost without thinking, so I could focus on the emotion and artistry of the piece.

The long hours sitting at the piano after school eventually led to my biggest recital with the city's orchestra, and instead of losing myself in the technicalities of each movement, I was able to move with the music, my fingers flying as if they had a life of their own.

Practice formed the muscle memory I needed when it was time to take the stage, and the same goes for wisdom.

Whatever wisdom we've gained so far in this Bible study— understanding the knowledge we have about God, listening to the Holy Spirit, looking for God in the midst of hardships, and learning through community—can be repeated and then built upon.

Let's say you learned to look for God in the middle of a deep depression due to loss. You noticed His kindness and attention toward you in the smallest ways when you didn't feel like anyone else understood or saw your pain. In the depths of despair, God was there through His silent comfort and provision through community.

The next time you go through loss and experience a similar depression, you may instinctually remember how you felt in God's presence.

By building muscle memories of trust and faithful obedience, we can withstand the trials that test our faith when they come.

It won't change the enormity of the pain, but you can recall that God did not leave you or abandon you in your worst moment. You practice what you learned the first time around—repeating truths and reaching out to others for prayer. And though you're still hurting, you have an assurance of hope you couldn't pinpoint before. You know with more certainty than before that God can and will carry you through.

As we practice the wisdom we've gained both in our everyday moments and in our most difficult seasons, we become wiser and sturdier in our faith. Even when the waves are relentless, we know to find our footing on the rock of Christ, because in Him we will not be overcome.

Read Proverbs 3:11–12. Consider the word *discipline* here not as punishment but as development and instruction that move us toward progress. If you've ever felt like God's discipline can be harsh, how does this passage change your view of Him?

SCRIPTURE MEMORY MOMENT

Write out Matthew 7:24–25. What wisdom do you need to put into practice this week?

A PRAYER FOR TODAY

LORD, *thank You for the purpose behind repetition and practice and that You don't require it simply because You want good behavior from me. It's for my discipline, my learning, and my wisdom, so I can mature in faith. Help me build on what You've already taught me so far. Thank You for Christ, my firm foundation, the rock on which I can stand. Amen.*

DAY 3

Train yourself to be godly. For physical training is of some value, but godliness has value for all things, holding promise for both the present life and the life to come.

1 Timothy 4:7–8

What comes to mind when you think of the phrase "spiritual disciplines"?

_____

_____

_____

_____

As we strive to become more like Jesus, seeking wisdom and building our lives on His foundation, we develop spiritual muscle memory by being disciplined. Again, let's reframe the word _discipline_ to mean practicing with intention or training. We become wise by putting into practice the wisdom we've gained, our goal being maturity in faith.

Though there are general spiritual practices, or disciplines, that we find in Scripture and observe in the church, what works a certain way for one person might not work for you. Some practices can be greatly beneficial in one season but less effective in another. You might discover that your go-to practices continue to draw you into God's presence every single time, or you might find that you have to approach the practices from a different angle as you grow.

The point of spiritual disciplines is to grow closer to God and be transformed into Christ's likeness, so as we go through some practices today, think about how you can make them work for you. Take the basic principle and figure out a way to apply it in your current season or try a new approach you haven't explored before.

Also, remember that a spiritual discipline must be practiced with intention for it to bear fruit in your life. Find a way to make it happen consistently with rhythms or routines. And since we're often prone to perfectionism or legalism, check in with yourself as you practice to make sure your goal is growth, not achievement—the goal is Jesus, not self-improvement. Knowing how to do all this will be by trial and error, wisdom, and the Holy Spirit.

So take a deep breath in, deep breath out. Imagine God ready to walk with you and cover you with grace. Then open your hands to receive what He wants to teach you today.

> Philippians 2:6–7 tells us that Jesus, "being in very nature God, did not consider equality with God something to be used to his own advantage; rather, he made himself nothing by taking the very nature of a servant, being made in human likeness." Now, keeping that in mind, look up Luke 2:40, 52. What does the Luke passage tell you about growing in grace and wisdom and how God is with us as we do?

Make sure your goal is growth, not achievement—the goal is Jesus, not self-improvement.

What have you learned about spiritual disciplines from your church? Which ones are practiced most within your community, and which ones do you find easiest to practice consistently in your life?

A quick Google search will show you that there are various lists and categories of spiritual disciplines. You can find many books written on each discipline, with new ones being published every year. So if you want to dig deeper into some of the practices we discuss, there's a wealth of information you can dive into!

For our purposes today, we'll cover the basic principles of four specific spiritual disciplines and various ways you can practice them. There are other practices that are just as important, such as fasting, soul friendships, or worship, so consider this list abbreviated for the sake of time and space.

Reading and Studying God's Word

You're doing it right now, plain and simple: you're reading and studying God's Word on the topic of wisdom. Through it, you're learning more about God and wrestling with challenging truths. As you engage with God's written word to you, He shows you new or deeper revelations, and even when you feel as though nothing fresh was revealed to you, time spent with Him in the Word is never wasted.

You can spend time each day reading by yourself, or you can go through an in-depth Bible study with your church small group. Plenty of Bible reading plans are available for you to follow, and nowadays you can even listen to an audio version of the Bible. It might take more effort on some days, or you might have stretches of time when you have the capacity to linger longer. Figure out ways you can be reading and studying God's Word in this season of your life.

Prayer and Listening

Prayer is conversing with God on an intimate level, sharing as you might to a safe friend, asking for help as from a loving parent, and listening for His voice or for the Spirit to nudge you. Just as God speaks to us through His Word, He also communicates to us through the Holy Spirit. Sometimes He does this by bringing someone to mind whom we can pray for or by giving us an answer to something we've been praying about. Other times He does this by convicting us of something we did that we didn't even realize was hurtful or wrong.

For most of my adult life, I wrote out my prayers in my journal, filling scores of them over the years. Nowadays prayer looks like short "Help!," "Have mercy," or "Thank you" prayers offered throughout the day whenever something comes up (or whenever the Spirit reminds me). When words fail us, sometimes all we can do is trust that the Holy Spirit and Jesus intercede on our behalf (Rom. 8:26–27, 34). However we communicate with God, He longs to listen and speak to us in return.

Sabbath and Rhythms of Rest

Sabbath is intentionally resting from work and from the busyness of life. When God created the world, He rested on the seventh day (Gen. 2:2)—a whole day to cease work and delight in what He had done. In following God's pattern, we pause our laboring and rest for a day during the week. It is for the benefit of our whole being—physical, mental, emotional, and spiritual—and for us to remember that we are not bound to any hustle, to any system, to anyone but the Lord.

Though a day of Sabbath is generally encouraged, some life circumstances may prevent taking a whole day of rest. I think about families who run small businesses that have to be open seven days a week or single parents who have to work two jobs to care for their family, adult children who are caring full-time for their aging parents or parents of children with special needs who rarely have a whole day at their disposal.

Still, God invites us all to rest, and though it may not be an entire day or even two consecutive hours, we can implement rhythms of rest throughout our days. This can be as simple as taking five minutes to practice deep breathing while praying, "Help me, God." Or it can look like sleeping the full amount of hours your body needs to function well. It can be setting boundaries by saying no to people or opportunities that drain you and keeping your schedule more open. Whether it's a whole day or a couple of minutes, we can be intentional about resting with God.

Celebration and Delight

Celebrating what God has done and delighting in God and His creation is a spiritual discipline we rarely learn about. However, from the beginning, God delighted in what He made (Gen. 1:4), and He delights in us as His children (Ps. 147:11; Zeph. 3:17). When we see evidence of His work in our lives, we celebrate by pausing, worshiping, jumping up and down, or sharing our testimony of His faithfulness with others.

Our celebration and delight in God can be expressed through a party praising Him for His goodness, with a tangible token to always remind ourselves that He cares, or through art—drawn, sung, written, or filmed. As Philippians 4:4 reminds us, "Rejoice in the Lord always. I will say it again: Rejoice!"

Practicing these spiritual disciplines leads to wisdom as we live our lives in the presence of God. As we do, may we taste and see how good God really is (Ps. 34:8).

> **Choose one spiritual discipline that we discussed today. How do you plan to practice it this week?**

_____

_____

_____

_____

SCRIPTURE MEMORY MOMENT

Read and write out Matthew 7:24–25 three times. Consider how practicing spiritual disciplines builds our wisdom muscles.

A PRAYER FOR TODAY

GOD, *thank You for these disciplines that nourish my whole being. Help me find rhythms that work. I pray that I'll be able to keep at them consistently while also being flexible enough not to lock myself into legalism or perfectionism. When I lose motivation, show me how this leads to wisdom in the long run but also for my everyday life. Amen.*

DAY 4

How does practicing wisdom, which we gain through all the ways we've learned about these past four weeks, lead to trusting God more?

_____

_____

_____

_____

When my kids first learned to walk, they would pause after each step, unsure if they should take another. I'd clap and cheer them on as if they were Olympic athletes, and my enthusiasm encouraged them to take one more wobbly step, then another, until they reached my embrace.

When they first learned to ride a bike, they gripped the handlebars with fear in their eyes and wobbled down the street, stopping every few seconds to catch themselves so they wouldn't fall. When I held their seat and ran alongside them, fear melted into joy and freedom, knowing they'd be held steady with me by their side.

We learn to trust when a regular repetition of courageous faith and risk is met with love and steadfastness. With people, there is always potential for disappointment and heartbreak, but with God, we have a foundation in Christ that's secure.

This, of course, doesn't mean that we're shielded from doubt, illnesses, or disillusionment. Many of us have stories of unexpected autoimmune diseases or cancer, betrayal by people we trust, and misgivings about faith, God, and the church because of our experience with toxic leaders. Learning to trust God through or after these traumatic experiences may take years or may feel impossible.

The rock of Christ can handle that. He won't shake or crumble or push us off the ledge because we're not holding on tightly enough. *He* holds *us*, anchoring our hearts so we can weather the storms that are guaranteed to come.

As we take steps of faith, practice wisdom, and grow in trust over and over again, the return is that we gain more of each in abundance.

> **Read Psalm 69:1–2, then Psalm 40:1–5. How have you experienced the anchoring that's made possible because of Christ? Or how do you need God to do that for you now?**

> **Read Hebrews 11:1–3 and Proverbs 3:5–6. If faith is being certain of what we can't see, how do we learn to trust God? What helps us put our trust in Him?**

Trusting by faith seems contrary to logic. To many people it might seem foolish or even childish to believe in something you can't see. This is why we stop believing in Santa Claus or the tooth fairy once we grow up—or once someone shatters the magic for us as kids. But as Hebrews 11:1 says, "Faith is . . . assurance about what we do not see." Having faith isn't foolish if the object of our faith is trustworthy, and God is worthy of our trust because He has proven Himself to be.

Consider how God promised a Savior to redeem the world after Adam and Eve sinned in the garden of Eden (Gen. 3) and then centuries later fulfilled that promise in Jesus:

> For God so loved the world that he gave his one and only Son, that whoever believes in him shall not perish but have eternal life. For God did not send his Son into the world to condemn the world, but to save the world through him. (John 3:16–17)

God's greatest promise to redeem the world back to Himself came true in Christ's death and resurrection.

And do you remember how God answered the Israelites' cries to be saved from enslavement in Egypt? God sent Moses to free them and then provided for them in the wilderness through multiple miracles.

In my own life, when I didn't think I could ever be truly seen and loved in my marriage, God sent little reminders that *He* saw me and loved me. These often came in the form of random bouquets of peonies from friends.

In each of these stories (including my marriage), it took years for the deliverance and breakthrough to come. Yet through the waiting and in the outcome, God was the answer. He was the reward. He was with us. And He was working on our behalf. He was everything.

His timing and ways are mysterious, and coupled with the realities of this world, they can be frustrating to figure out or understand. But He is trustworthy. And rather than just taking my word for it, I pray you can see that His trustworthiness spans all history, from the very beginning of time all the way to the ins and outs of your life too.

Sometimes our pain and trauma keep us from being able to trust God. Rather than telling us to hide them, God wants to hear them. Use this template to write crying-out prayers. Repeat as many times as you need to.

God, I'm having a hard time trusting You because _____ _____ . *Show me that You are trustworthy, and help me believe.*

_____

_____

_____

_____

As our trust in God builds, it becomes easier to obey Him—and to obey Him more quickly. Not only that, but when we see that God is not limited by us, our vision, or even our imagination, we understand that the possibilities are beyond what we can fathom.

Now, this might feel overwhelming because vastness could mean not having a plan or not knowing all the options. But God's trustworthiness gives us the freedom to release our desire for control and to be curious—even excited—about what He can do. We can come to a place where we wholeheartedly obey without knowing everything because we trust Him!

As our Scripture passage for today says in Proverbs 3:5, wisdom is trusting the Lord with all our heart and not depending on our own understanding of things. Listen to wisdom's invitation; on the other side of it is steadiness of faith, awe of God, and nearness to Him.

> **How has your desire for control limited your trust in God? Give an example from your life.**

SCRIPTURE MEMORY MOMENT

Write out Matthew 7:24–25. As you do, remember that Christ is our firm foundation. He is trustworthy.

A PRAYER FOR TODAY

LORD, *thank You for being trustworthy, a God of Your word. You don't waver or run hot or cold in Your love for me. Thank You that I don't have to understand everything or be in control in order to walk in Your way. When I become anxious that I can't see Your plan or what the next step of obedience should be, help me pause and remember that You will show me in Your good timing. Increase my faith, my trust, and my peace in You. Amen.*

Simon Peter answered him, "Lord, to whom shall we go? You have the words of eternal life. We have come to believe and to know that you are the Holy One of God."

John 6:68–69

Reflect on what we've learned this week about practicing wisdom and building our spiritual muscle memory. How does practicing wisdom through trust and obedience then lead to having a lasting faith?

Growing in our faith is less like a straight line moving up and to the right along a graph and more like a journey through a story. There are times when the path is clearly defined and we walk confidently with God. There are wilderness seasons when nothing makes sense, when the truths you know don't feel true or even real. Some days you'll feel so near to God you can't imagine how it could be otherwise, and other days you'll wonder if He's abandoned you in your suffering or loneliness. Even in the everyday, you may experience ups and downs. Your path probably won't look like anyone else's, and all of this is part of the journey.

Instead of despairing every time we sin or make unwise choices or don't live perfectly, growing in wisdom helps us take the long view of where we're headed. Our growth isn't measured like a behavior chart for children. Our growth is the fruit of God's love and grace at work in us and of us working out our faith through obedience to become more like Christ (Phil. 2:12–13).

One evidence of maturing faith is wisdom. Therefore, our practice of wisdom will keep us growing and will result in a faith that carries us for the long haul. Like the parable of the talents in Matthew 25:14–30, when we steward well what God gives us—in this case, by living out wisdom—we gain more, as God desires us to. This keeps us going, able to carry on until we meet with God face-to-face one day.

The journey may be long, but we can have a faith that goes the distance, that becomes fuller and deeper as we continue to practice the wisdom we've learned along the way.

Read Matthew 25:14–30. What is the context for this parable (see Matt. 24:3)? How does that perspective help you see the importance of being committed to practicing wisdom?

Think of someone whose faith lasted for the long haul. What are some of the characteristics they have that you admire and wish you had for your life?

As we journey further along in our faith, consistent practice of wisdom is bound to produce fruit. Galatians 5:22–23 says, "But the fruit of the Spirit is love, joy, peace, patience, kindness, goodness, faithfulness, gentleness, self-control; against such things there is no law" (ESV). And even in our suffering, consistent practice can bear hope and perseverance (Rom. 5:1–5). Wisdom can be seen through each of these aspects. For example, loving others in wisdom can look like having clear boundaries, as Kristen Strong shared about in week 2. Faithfulness in wisdom can look like discovering that God's presence is what we need most in the midst of struggle and pain, as Michele Cushatt shared in week 3. Today, as we look at faith for the long haul, let's talk about what patience and perseverance in wisdom look like.

Patience is being able to do something without getting anxious, flustered, or angered by the process. I'll be the first to admit that I struggle with patience because I don't like the lack of control over an outcome. I want to have a hand in how a decision is made or what direction my life will take. I'm impatient to see what's around the corner so I can know what I need to do in the present. But as wisdom has led to trust and obedience, which have then led to more trust and further obedience, I've seen that we don't have to rush—through life, through growth, through grief, through anything. God is not impatient. He is not in a rush for us to arrive at a better place. Even though God's pace might seem slow, He has the view of eternity, and therefore His tempo is the one we want to follow.

Patience braided with wisdom looks like peace. Even though we can't see the bigger picture, we can patiently and faithfully take the next step of obedience because we can trust that God knows what He's doing. We can be confident that we're not behind in His plan for our lives. Patience keeps our dependence on God, believing that He will provide daily for what we need.

I still struggle with impatience, but instead of feeling restless to figure out God's vision and purpose for my life, I can rest in His goodness, sovereignty, and love. I don't need to rush getting to the next level or achieving the next goal. Wisdom has taught me to wait and trust, to be patient and delight in finding God right where I am.

> **Read 2 Peter 3:8–9. What does this passage tell you about God's patience and His perspective on time and timing?**

To have a long-haul faith, we need perseverance. And perseverance in wisdom looks like tenacity and resilience. Struggle, loss, and pain are natural teachers for this, as are long seasons of waiting (for which we need both patience and perseverance). When the tunnel stretches farther than we'd like, holding our breath until we're out of the dark won't work. Wisdom teaches us how to persevere by holding on to life, joy, and God in the middle of the tunnel even as we walk toward the hope of light at the end of it.

> Wisdom teaches us how to persevere by holding on to life, joy, and God in the middle of the tunnel even as we walk toward the hope of light at the end of it.

Tenacity comes from the wisdom we learn by planting our feet firmly on the foundation we have in Christ. Every time we put that wisdom into practice, we're strengthened, less prone to being tossed back and forth by the waves and becoming unmoored.

Resilience comes from the wisdom we learn by being realistic yet hopeful in the midst of pain. We learn to celebrate and look for joy even when nothing is going right. This is not glossing over or denying our pain, which is never helpful, but being grounded in Christ to see that we can—we must—find reasons to rejoice when things are hard. Wisdom teaches us that we can hold both joy and pain, and that's how we keep going.

When we persevere far enough along in our faith, we see the same truth we've touched on several times through this study: God is all we've got.

In John 6:67–69, after many who had followed Jesus desert Him, He asks His disciples, "You do not want to leave too, do you?" Then Simon Peter answers, "Lord, to whom shall we go? You have the words of eternal life. We have come to believe and to know that you are the Holy One of God."

To whom shall we go?

As we practice wisdom through all of life's circumstances, we see repeatedly that God is everything we'll ever need. Nothing and no one can compare to Him. To whom shall we go? Wisdom says, "Stay with and cling to Him alone."

May we listen to wisdom's words and not give up practicing what we've learned from her.

Look up Psalm 73:25–26. How are you encouraged by this passage?

_____

_____

_____

_____

SCRIPTURE MEMORY MOMENT

Test yourself on Matthew 7:24–25. Try to say it out loud or write it from memory. As we move into the next week of our study, continue to reflect on these words.

A PRAYER FOR TODAY

GOD, *where would I be without You? Thank You that I have You and that You don't let me go. Teach me to apply wisdom in every part of my life and not tire of practicing it. Keep me grounded in You, and may my life bear much fruit as I stay rooted in You. Amen.*

WISDOM IS LEARNED OVER A LIFETIME

Wherever we are in life, no matter our age, we will always need wisdom. There's no final destination at which to arrive, no amount we could gain that would be too much. Perhaps that can be a comfort to us, knowing that we don't need to strive for our worth or a status in wisdom. We are perpetual learners, listening and responding to wisdom's call.

In the process of growing wise, one of the joys we have is to see how it changes us and others. As you read this opening story from (in)courage writer Patricia Raybon, consider how wisdom learned over a lifetime blooms, getting more beautiful as time passes.

A Story of Learning Wisdom

The first thing I noticed on the Zoom call was that everybody was younger than me. This was a group of women brought together from around the world to be part of a project. I felt excited by the work, which I was enjoying—my little part of it anyway.

Then I learned we'd all be meeting monthly to build a community so participants would feel connected. My introvert alarm bell started to ring.

Talk to people I don't know? Couldn't I just do my part of the project and mail it in?

In fact, no.

I began to worry. As the oldest of this young group—some barely in their twenties—I felt put on the spot to fulfill that daunting command from the book of Titus: "Older women likewise . . . train the young women" (2:3–4 ESV).

Sitting there, however, looking at twenty or so beautiful faces, each in her own Zoom box, I knew I wasn't ready. Teach these amazing women how to be wise? The pressure chilled me.

But getting older often presents this challenge. When younger Christian women meet me and see that I'm older, they suddenly defer to me, as if I'll open my mouth and pearls of sage wisdom will roll naturally off my tongue.

Thus, one younger friend calls me "Queen." On telephone calls, many of them refer to me as "ma'am," making me feel five hundred years old. I haven't figured out how to tell these beautiful people that, although I may appear older, age is just a number. Even more, it doesn't mean wisdom has come along for the ride.

In fact, I've been surprised how growing older confirms just how much I still haven't learned. I once heard that exact same thing from the oldest woman of my longtime church, who was about 101 at the time. She'd called me to chat about her latest book—yes, she was working on another one—and during our chat, she laughed about the surprises of old age.

"I'm amazed at what I still don't know," she said. She meant life lessons—those things that old age should convey just by virtue of living longer. "You never stop learning. I thought if I lived to 100, I'd have all of life figured out. But here I am at 101, still learning new things every day." She laughed. "Who knew?"

God knew. When it comes to wisdom, God *is* wisdom. As James 1:5 puts it, "If any of you lacks wisdom, you should ask God." We should ask God—not the 101-year-old lady at church who may be older but, like me, may still be learning things she never mastered. (She lived a vibrant life until age 107.)

Wisdom is indeed that lofty. That must be one reason Paul wrote his letter to Titus. Aware that he wouldn't live forever, Paul urged Titus to prepare wise leaders to carry on his example as well.

Paul had poured godly wisdom and maturity into Titus over many years, teaching, training, and developing him into a responsible, effective, wise leader. But he doesn't stop there. Paul instructs Titus to teach and train others—especially older people. "Teach the older men to be temperate, worthy of respect, self-controlled, and sound in faith, in love and in endurance" (Titus 2:2). Why? Because wisdom has to be taught—to everybody, regardless of age.

For my part, I'd been worried for years that when I reached a certain age, I'd be expected to teach and train younger women. I worried because nobody had ever taught me with intention how to be wise. I'd never had a mentor, nor had I spent intentional time studying wisdom for its own sake. I'd never sat myself down to learn as much as possible about life and how to live it—not only for the sake of succeeding at life but for the purpose of being wise.

I once learned that the word *wise* shares its root with the Latin word *videre*, meaning "to see." So the wise look after, guard, and guide others because they're visionary. Paul understood this process and thus told Titus to teach those who were older. Only then can they train the younger to be wise.

I reflect on this now and see that I'd missed the process completely. I'd overlooked how Paul makes no assumption that older folks will be wise because of their age. Instead, that's why Paul tells Titus to teach those who are older. They also need to learn so they can pass that learning to those who are younger.

I read the verses again, and I can't explain how I'd overlooked them. But the time has come for me to follow James's bold advice: "If any of you lacks wisdom, you should ask God" (1:5).

I feel skittish as I prepare to pray that prayer. If I ask for wisdom, will some life upheaval follow? Can't I gain wisdom without the add-on of some bumpy ride?

Then I remember the story of Bartimaeus (Mark 10:46–52). He was suffering from blindness, and when Jesus asked him, "What do you want me to do for you?" Bartimaeus boldly replied, "Rabbi, I want to see."

That's what I want too—not so that I'll be called Queen but so that others may know Christ as King because of the wisdom I show them.

Do you want that too? Then simply ask, "Lord, make me wise." He will kindly answer with a yes. From there, may we stay close, follow His way, and teach others to see Him too.

—PATRICIA RAYBON

Since age doesn't come with wisdom, what does that teach you about the importance of asking for wisdom and practicing it throughout your life?

In what ways do you see wisdom in yourself now, and in what ways do you see that you need more wisdom?

Read Proverbs 3:13–18. How does this passage describe the life of a wise person?

_____

_____

_____

_____

SCRIPTURE MEMORY MOMENT

This week's memory verse is Proverbs 19:8. Write the verse in your journal or on an index card (from the NIV as printed here or from your favorite translation.) Throughout the week, commit these words to memory as you seek to live a life of wisdom from here on out.

The one who gets wisdom loves life;
the one who cherishes understanding will soon
prosper.

A PRAYER FOR TODAY

GOD, *thank You that I can ask for wisdom and You will answer with a yes! I don't have to worry about needing to know everything by a certain point in my life. I can live and grow, trusting You will give the wisdom I need when I need it. Help me pay attention to those You want me to come alongside and learn from right now. I ask for wisdom. Amen.*

DAY 2

Instruct the wise and they will be wiser still;
teach the righteous and they will add to their learning.

Proverbs 9:9

What measures can you take to stay open, willing, and humble enough so you can keep learning from wisdom?

_____

_____

_____

_____

Ecclesiastes 7:23–24 says, "All this I tested by wisdom and I said, 'I am determined to be wise'—but this was beyond me. Whatever exists is far off and most profound—who can discover it?" Wisdom is too big and our lives too short to fully comprehend or gain all it has to teach us. But this doesn't mean we throw caution to the wind and live foolishly. Read the rest of Proverbs and Ecclesiastes, and you'll see that choosing to live wisely is better.

Further, our memory verse for this week says, "The one who gets wisdom loves life; the one who cherishes understanding will soon prosper" (Prov. 19:8). To understand more fully what that means, let's look at other translations for a different angle. The ESV translates it as, "Whoever gets sense loves his own soul; he who keeps understanding will discover good." The NLT says, "To acquire wisdom is to love yourself; people who cherish understanding will prosper."

To become wise, then, is to love yourself well, to care for your soul. Wisdom doesn't only pertain to the daily decisions we need to make; it is the kind of life we choose to live. Wisdom forms our lives and the people we become, and the more wisdom we gain, the more we realize how little we know and how that can actually be a good thing.

Though we're nearing the end of this study, in many ways this may be just the beginning of God creating in you a heart of wisdom. Let this be a lifelong work for you, and let's keep going.

> **Look up Ecclesiastes 2:13–14 and 7:11–12. In the midst of calling everything meaningless, how does the author still confirm that wisdom is worth pursuing?**

> **As you keep going in the pursuit of wisdom, are there any barriers that make you fear or doubt the journey or dread the work? If so, bring them into the light by telling them to God in prayer. Be specific as to why you might be feeling that way. Write your prayer below.**

The irony of becoming wiser is that as we understand more, we sometimes know less. The phrase "I don't know" is not a sign of weakness, ignorance, or stupidity. Instead, it can be a powerful acknowledgment of our limitations and our desire to humbly learn from others. Anytime we don't know what to say or do, we have an opportunity to point ourselves and others to the ultimate source of wisdom: God Himself.

As a leader, mentor, and parent, I've felt the pressure to always have the correct answer or wise advice for anyone who comes to me with their questions. Put in the spotlight, I'd scan my years of Bible learning, theological training, and life experiences to figure out the best response. Many times I simply regurgitated what I had been taught without taking into consideration what the Spirit might be saying in that particular moment. If anything, I trusted that the information I was giving was biblical truth that could work in any situation.

While it may have been helpful to some, I look back now and see that many of the things I once taught or shared with others were completely wrong. At other times, my lack of discernment didn't empower people to make their own decisions, or it set them up for disappointment in their relationship with God.

When I began struggling with how to explain difficult life circumstances to my children, I realized that "I don't know" can suffice. "I don't know" can bring us to the same place of learning, curiosity, vulnerability, and growth. Whether with my children, my mentees, or even for myself, that understanding freed me from the unrealistic expectation that I should know better because I'm older, more educated, or further along in my faith journey.

Remember what we learned in week 1? Knowledge doesn't always equal wisdom. When we don't know or understand something, it doesn't disqualify us from being wise. Instead, hitting the limits of our finite perspective is an invitation for us to inquire of God and to trust Him when things still don't make sense.

Being able to admit and accept "I don't know" as a legitimate answer to a question can be the wisest thing we can do. We can follow up by learning more to better understand the situation or by listening to the Holy Spirit to see how we might meet the needs of the person who sought us out. We can stay in the tension of not knowing while seeking wisdom from God's Word and our communities.

We always have room to grow in wisdom, to unlearn so we can learn, to be wrong and be met by grace.

> **What keeps you from admitting you don't know something? How do you follow up when you don't know? Is it a wise response?**

There are some things in life we will never know the answers to. However, on the flip side of saying "I don't know" is the responsibility we have to keep learning what we can. This is especially important when our lack of knowledge is because of ignorance, lack of exposure, or wrong teaching. For example, in talking to my children about death and racism, I've had to research and figure out how to have these conversations with them in an age-appropriate way. Glossing over the hard truths wasn't an option, because we were facing these issues in real life and my kids needed help to handle them.

So I read books, listened to parents who had gone before me, and did the best I could to pass on what I learned to my kids. The

Being able to admit and accept "I don't know" as a legitimate answer to a question can be the wisest thing we can do.

conversations weren't (and still aren't) easy or always productive, but we are finding our way through as we go.

When God shows us that our "I don't know" is a nudge *to* know, let's not reject His teaching or deny our ignorance. Proverbs 12:1 says (not so gently), "Whoever loves discipline loves knowledge, but whoever hates correction is stupid."

Let's not be foolish, friends. Instead, let's keep choosing wisdom—for with it, we will care for our own souls.

> **Read Proverbs 15:31–33. When we realize that something we thought we knew is in fact wrong, what course of action should we take?**

SCRIPTURE MEMORY MOMENT

Write out Proverbs 19:8. As you do, consider how growing in wisdom is a way to care for your soul.

A PRAYER FOR TODAY

LORD, *thank You for the grace of being able to say "I don't know." Thank You that it's not an indictment on my character or intelligence but an acknowledgment that I'm human. I pray for wisdom in knowing what to do after that admission. I don't want to stop at not knowing; I want to keep growing in knowledge and understanding and in discernment by listening to the Holy Spirit's guidance. I trust You when there are no answers. I trust You when things don't make sense. I trust You to give me wisdom every day of my life. Amen.*

DAY 3

If any of you lacks wisdom, you should ask God, who gives generously to all without finding fault, and it will be given to you.

James 1:5

When you look back at the times you've prayed and asked God for wisdom, how did you discern between His wisdom and human wisdom?

_____

_____

_____

_____

For the past five weeks, we've been discussing various ways we can learn to be wise. We gain wisdom by understanding knowledge, listening to the Holy Spirit, experiencing difficulty, being in community, and practicing the wisdom we've learned. A lifetime of practice will strengthen our faith, deepen our trust and intimacy with God, and help us become familiar with His voice, His character, and His ways.

Our ability to discern wisdom becomes more refined as we practice over a lifetime. I imagine it's like gaining a more sophisticated taste palate.

Growing up, I loved it when my parents would order a McDonald's cheeseburger Happy Meal for me. What kid doesn't like receiving a toy with their food that comes in a box shaped like a tiny house? It was a meal and a treat combined in one, and I relished it. Once I became older, I started ordering the two-cheeseburger combo meal because it was the taste I was accustomed to and liked, and over time the #9 became my go-to stress food.

When I married my husband, who was a professional chef back then and had grown up hardly ever eating at McDonald's, I couldn't understand or appreciate the quality of food he cooked at home. He used carefully chosen, fresh ingredients, and cooking from scratch was a given. All of it felt unnecessarily fancy and inefficient for me. To me, getting full for the cheapest price possible was the goal.

Slowly, I began to differentiate between bad and good, good and better. McDonald's cheeseburgers started to lose their appeal, and eventually I learned to cook from scratch like my husband, which helped refine my palate even more. (Don't worry, I still eat a #9 every once in a while.) I needed to taste and see what was good in order to recognize and appreciate what truly good food tasted like.

And so it is with wisdom. The more we taste and see that God's wisdom is right and best, the better we can discern it from human wisdom. We learn to distinguish between the two by comparing the wisdom we receive to God's Word and specifically to Jesus.

> Read James 3:13–18. Write down the characteristics of unspiritual wisdom and the characteristics of the wisdom that comes from heaven.

The more we taste and see that God's wisdom is right and best, the better we can discern it from human wisdom.

In what ways do you see the characteristics of heavenly wisdom in the person and life of Jesus?

Distinguishing between godly wisdom and human wisdom is easier when it's between good and bad choices. When one choice stems from envy or selfish ambition, as stated in James 3:14–16, we know it's not true wisdom. Of course, if we're in deep denial of our envy or selfish ambition, we might get confused even between good and bad choices. If that's the case, we can ask ourselves some basic questions to make sure we're not getting in our own way of true wisdom:

1. Does this choice reflect the way Jesus lived?
2. Am I willing to bring this to my trusted community? Or if I did, would there be hesitation, shame, or guilt attached to it? (Make sure the shame and guilt aren't coming from a place of legalism.) Do I feel resistance to hearing what they might share with me?
3. Am I mentally, emotionally, spiritually, and physically well? (When we aren't well in one of these areas, all the others are affected, thus potentially clouding our judgment.)
4. How does this choice line up with what God has been teaching me? If you're not sure what He's been teaching you, then ask yourself how this choice lines up with the truths of God's Word (see James 3:17).

Now, when we're trying to distinguish between good and better or better and best, it might not be outrightly clear which choice is wise. Let's say both choices reflect Jesus's love and our community is split between what we should do. We're healthy and well in our spirit, and either choice could line up with what God is teaching us. What do we do then?

Along our faith journey, there will be times when the choice is up to us. God doesn't always make it crystal clear what He wants us to do but entrusts us to step in whichever direction we choose. God made us with desires, ambitions, and dreams, along with thoughts, feelings, a personality, and a conscience or gut that can help us make decisions. He also gave us the Holy Spirit who lives within us to guide us with courage and peace to be wise. Lastly, we have the wisdom He's taught us through experience to build on.

Here are some further questions that might be helpful to ask yourself if needed:

1. Is this the right season or time in my life for this choice?
2. How does this choice fit into what God is doing around me in my family, relationships, church, or community?
3. Even though I feel afraid, is this something that God is inviting me into as a way of stretching my faith, deepening my trust, or expanding my view of Him and/or others?
4. Does this choice affirm a pattern of what God's been saying to me over the past several months?

God gives us wisdom, makes us wiser, and entrusts us with the wisdom He's given us. It's part gift, part practice, and part faith. But the promise of James 1:5 is a guarantee: "If any of you lacks wisdom, you should ask God, who gives generously to all without finding fault, and it will be given to you."

Ask away, friends.

Read James 1:6–8. What do you think this passage means with regard to asking for wisdom?

_____

_____

_____

_____

Let's end today on this thought: when we ask God for wisdom, we must ask with the intention of believing and acting upon the wisdom He gives us. Asking only to then doubt His wisdom is like being "blown and tossed by the wind" (James 1:6). It shows that we didn't intend to obey or that we don't trust God, thus making us wishy-washy, or "double-minded" and "unstable" (v. 8).

The promise of James 1:5 remains true no matter what: God will give us wisdom generously. What we do with it and how we live it determines whether we become wise. So, yes, let's ask away, but let's also make sure we're ready to follow through on the wisdom He gives us.

SCRIPTURE MEMORY MOMENT

Read and write out Proverbs 19:8 three times. As you do, think about how wisdom can lead to flourishing.

A PRAYER FOR TODAY

GOD, *thank You that when I ask for wisdom, You answer without holding back. Teach me to discern between Your wisdom and human wisdom, especially when everything sounds right. Holy Spirit, guide me in those moments when I need to choose between good and better. Help me trust You, and thank You for entrusting me to make wise choices with the mind, heart, and experiences You've given me. I want more of You, God—to know You, love You, and follow after You. Amen.*

DAY 4

Walk with the wise and become wise,
for a companion of fools suffers harm.
Proverbs 13:20

Have you ever been mentored, or have you mentored someone else? What kind of wisdom did you gain from those experiences?

Over a lifetime, we will find ourselves in communities that shift and grow and in friendships that come and go. We discussed in week 4 that it's a gift to be able to see and experience God more and to gain wisdom we otherwise wouldn't have through others. No matter what season of life we're in, no matter how young or old we are, we need others and they need us. As we all try to figure out how to live this life, we benefit from walking closely with those who are wiser than us and also passing on our wisdom to those who want to learn from us.

Mentorship is intentionally and mutually investing in a relationship with someone you want to learn from or teach. It can be synonymous with discipleship when it happens in a faith context, and whenever we can mentor or be mentored, it is a gift and a privilege.

Many of us may long to have a mentor but know that they're not easily found. We might go our whole lives wishing someone wiser would walk with us and never have anyone invest in us like that, or our circumstances might not allow us the time or flexibility or access we need to be mentored. Or perhaps it hasn't even crossed our minds to look for one or we're surrounded by people we don't consider mentor material.

Though we might not have opportunities for these intentional relationships in the way we hope, we can always learn from people who are wiser than us, whether that's through books and other media sources, leaders, speakers, the lady at church who always has a listening ear, or even younger generations. Wisdom can come from unlikely sources as well as obvious ones. So when we ask God for wisdom through mentors, we need to be on the lookout and be willing to learn from the people He sends our way.

Who are the mentors in your life and how have they influenced you? Name anyone you look up to or learn from and write a letter telling them what you've learned from them.

Read Hebrews 13:7. What can mentors provide for their mentees?

We can be mentored from afar by authors, preachers, or community leaders. Their words, passions, and example might be the only way we find the sort of mentoring we desire when our immediate circles and communities can't provide what we need. The beauty of our present time is that we have access to so many resources, and it's to our benefit, our growth in wisdom, that we make the most of them.

But when we have the privilege of finding mentors in our everyday proximity, we experience the advantage of learning by watching firsthand. When I was younger and learning to play piano, my teacher would try to explain how she wanted a certain part to sound. She'd describe how a note needed to be held just a tad longer to evoke a certain emotion. Though I conceptually understood what she meant, it wasn't until she played the part herself to demonstrate how it should sound that I was able to hear what she meant and then play it myself.

Sometimes the only way we learn is by modeling and imitating. When we are in community with wise people, we learn nuances of wisdom we might not learn otherwise. We get to see firsthand how we can respond with love when someone angers us or how to set healthy boundaries with our parents. We get to witness mistakes and failures up close and see how to get back up, how to ask for forgiveness, and how to live by grace alone. We learn from the unfiltered moments of real-life wisdom instead of the edited sound bites of wisdom found on social media.

Whomever we choose to mentor us, the most important criteria we should have for them is that their lives reflect Jesus's—not necessarily in piety but in love. As Paul says in 1 Corinthians 11:1, "Follow my example, as I follow the example of Christ." Jesus is the ultimate mentor for us and the greatest example we all should follow. He navigated unjust circumstances, family issues, and friends who couldn't be there in

His hardest moments, all while staying true to His purpose, His love for people, and His trust of God the Father. If we choose to imitate anyone, may we always choose to imitate Christ.

So let's take Proverbs 13:20 to heart and find ways to walk with the wise so we can become wiser. Let's have a teachable heart, willing and ready to learn from those who are further along the journey of wisdom.

> Read John 13:12–17 and Ephesians 5:1–2. In these Scripture passages, what kind of example did Jesus set for us?

As we grow in wisdom, we can become the wise ones whom others can walk with. Like we read in Patricia's story, even though we haven't had mentors ourselves, we may come to an age or a time in our lives when people look to us as examples they can follow. Then, whether we feel qualified or wise enough, God may invite us to mentor them, and it is our privilege to do so.

Wisdom gained should be shared, and whether or not we've had a mentor ourselves, we can become mentors who live by example and invest our time in others.

Several years ago, I started mentoring a group of young women in their late twenties and early thirties. None of them knew each other, but they were all hungry to be mentored, willing to commit to a mentorship, and teachable. We didn't have a curriculum or a book or an agenda to go through. Instead, I told them our goal was to walk through life with each other as Jesus had walked with the two disciples on the road to Emmaus in Luke 24. Slowly and at first a bit awkwardly, we shared what was going on in our lives, got to know one another, and created a space where we could practice our God-given gifts in a safe community. Over time, not only have I been able to impart the wisdom I've learned but they, too, have shared wisdom with each other and with me—and in doing so we have all pointed one another to Christ.

There isn't only one way of mentoring well, but in our group we've made sure to respect the following values to get the most from our time together:

1. We learn from each other. Though I'm their mentor, we all understand that God can and will speak through any one of us. This means that when the Holy Spirit prompts a word, an encouragement, or even a warning, we make sure to share.

2. We are committed to the community. Every six months, I have each woman evaluate whether she can stay committed to the group. This rhythm provides stability yet allows for changes that can happen as we go through different seasons in life.

3. Our investment in each other is for the other group members as much as it is for ourselves. We are in it for the long haul, walking together through difficult circumstances, cheering one another on, and celebrating our joys and victories together.

Walk with the wise and invite others to walk with you. Gain wisdom and share wisdom. As God gives generously to us, may we also give generously to others.

SCRIPTURE MEMORY MOMENT

Write out Proverbs 19:8. As you do, thank God for the mentors in your life. If you don't have a mentor, ask Him for one.

A PRAYER FOR TODAY

LORD, *thank You for the gift of mentorship. Thank You for providing people, relationships, and resources to keep me growing in wisdom. God, I pray for a mentor to walk with me in this season of my life. Keep my eyes open for the opportunity to invest in and mentor others so we can all become wiser together. Amen.*

DAY 5

The beginning of wisdom is this: Get wisdom.
Though it cost all you have, get understanding.

Proverbs 4:7

After everything we've learned in the past six weeks, how have you seen more evidence of wisdom in the way you live your life?

_____

_____

_____

_____

Wisdom is learned in morsels—like the manna God provided every morning for the Israelites as they wandered through the wilderness (Exod. 16). We can't gather more wisdom than we need and hoard it to avoid having to learn again. God gives us wisdom abundantly and yet in just the right amount to keep us growing and trusting Him. And, like manna, wisdom is both a gift and something we must get for ourselves if we want it.

When we ask God to create in us a heart of wisdom, it impacts every area of our life—from setting daily priorities to having boundaries in relationships; from how we manage stress and live with joy to how we look to the future and dream. Wisdom puts things into perspective for us and helps us answer this question: How then shall we live?

And with anything we learn in our faith, how we live should always point back to God. As we read yesterday in Ephesians 5:1–2, "Follow God's example, therefore, as dearly loved children and walk in the way of love, just as Christ loved us and gave himself up for us as a fragrant offering and sacrifice to God." As dearly loved children of God, we walk in the way of love and in the way of wisdom.

Further on in verses 15–17, Paul writes, "Be very careful, then, how you live—not as unwise but as wise, making the most of every opportunity, because the days are evil. Therefore do not be foolish, but understand what the Lord's will is." To live wisely, we must make the most of our time—both in our day-to-day and over a lifetime—living like Christ and understanding what God's will is so we can take part in the redemption story He began in the garden of Eden and that He is still writing even now. The way we do this will be different for each of us as the Spirit shows us how, but when we live by wisdom in every area of life, we don't waste time; we make the most of it.

Take a look at your daily or weekly calendar and evaluate: How busy are you? Do your scheduled activities and to-do lists reflect a life of love and wisdom? What about your monthly and yearly goals or your life values and priorities—do they reflect living like Christ? If not, what adjustments need to be made so that wisdom is tangibly reflected in how you live your life?

As we continue to grow wiser, we become both carriers and givers of wisdom. Proverbs 13:14 says, "The teaching of the wise is a fountain of life, turning a person from the snares of death." Whether or not we intentionally mentor others, people around us will be blessed by the wisdom we hold simply from being in our presence and watching how we live. The way we carry ourselves, the way we handle crises, the way we love, the way we speak up or stay quiet, the way we heal from past wounds, the way we hope—all this speaks volumes and gives life to those who witness it. A life of wisdom opens the door for heaven to break through here on earth because people will be able to see God in us.

These glimpses of the divine infuse us and others with hope. Wisdom gives us insight into how we can move forward through conflict, live through tragedy, and imagine new ways to create spaces in our world that reflect heaven on earth. The Holy Spirit gives us the perspective to see, believe, and trust with childlike faith as we become wiser, and isn't that the most beautiful paradox? As we mature in faith, we become more childlike in faith. Instead of fretting, we can hope and anticipate that God will make a way. Instead of becoming puffed up in our knowledge about God, we can confidently say "I don't know" and be okay with not being able to understand or solve all the mysteries of God. Instead of trying to be independent, we can rest in our dependence on God and one another. The paradoxes of our faith show us that God is all we need. He is the ultimate source of wisdom.

Becoming wise is a lifelong journey, but wisdom gives us the freedom to be in-process and to progress with grace because we are learning bit by bit. We don't need to rush through the journey, but we make the most of every day—not to get gold stars and pats on the back for

Wisdom gives us the freedom to be in-process and to progress with grace.

becoming wise but to get life. In Proverbs 8:35, wisdom says, "For those who find me find life and receive favor from the LORD."

Wisdom is always worth gaining.

> **Read Philippians 1:3–6. How does verse 6 encourage you in your journey of wisdom?**

Finally, as our passage for today says, "The beginning of wisdom is this: Get wisdom. Though it cost all you have, get understanding" (Prov. 4:7). God is creating in you a heart of wisdom *as you pursue wisdom.* You pray and ask God for wisdom, and He gives it to you *as you live it out.* It happens when you go get it. So, friends, let's make the most of our time by desiring wisdom, pursuing it, and living it out every single day of our lives.

> **What is one truth from this week that encourages you to keep going in your pursuit of wisdom?**

SCRIPTURE MEMORY MOMENT

Test yourself on Proverbs 19:8. Try to say it out loud or write it from memory. When you have time, go back through all six memory verses from this study, and continue to meditate on them as you move forward with a heart of wisdom.

A PRAYER FOR TODAY

GOD, *thank You for all You've taught me through this study and for faithfully continuing the work You've started in me. Thank You for the way You guide and lead me through Your wisdom. Holy Spirit, help me make the most of every day by living like Jesus, and keep me tender to Your movement so I can be quick to obey. I pray that I would live wisely and teach others to do the same. Lord, I ask for more wisdom. In Jesus's name I pray, amen.*

NOTES

Week 1 Wisdom Is Learned through Understanding Knowledge

1. Douglas Kelly and Philip Rollinson, *The Westminster Shorter Catechism in Modern English* (Phillipsburg, NJ: P&R, 1986), 5.

2. I learned this from Tracey Gee's Authentic Alignment course, https://traceygee.me/alignment.

3. Christina Morales and Allyson Waller, "A Gender-Reveal Celebration Is Blamed for a Wildfire. It Isn't the First Time," *New York Times*, September 7, 2020, https://www.nytimes.com/2020/09/07/us/gender-reveal-party-wildfire.html; Brian Rokos, "San Bernardino County's District Attorney's Office Weighs Possible Charges in El Dorado Fire," *The Sun*, January 15, 2021, https://www.sbsun.com/2021/01/15/san-bernardino-countys-district-attorney-weighs-possible-charges-in-el-dorado-fire/.

Week 2 Wisdom Is Learned through Listening

1. Gary Thomas, *When to Walk Away: Finding Freedom from Toxic People* (Grand Rapids: Zondervan, 2019), 37.

2. Thomas, *When to Walk Away*, 25.

3. John McKinley, "Metaphors Revealing the Holy Spirit, Part 2: The Wind as a Metaphor of the Holy Spirit," *The Good Book Blog*, November 18, 2015, https://www.biola.edu/blogs/good-book-blog/2015/metaphors-revealing-the-holy-spirit-part-two-the-wind-as-a-metaphor-of-the-holy-spirit.

Week 3 Wisdom Is Learned through Experience

1. "Meet Our Human Books," Human Library, accessed May 12, 2022, https://humanlibrary.org/meet-our-human-books/.

Week 4 Wisdom Is Learned through Community

1. National Ocean Service, "How Many Species Live in the Ocean?," accessed June 7, 2021, https://oceanservice.noaa.gov/facts/ocean-species.html.

2. I will use the word *diverseness* to describe variety and the word *diversity* in regards to different ethnic backgrounds.

3. This does not include staying in a community that is in any way abusive.

ABOUT THE AUTHORS

Grace P. Cho is a Korean American writer, poet, and speaker, and a senior acquisitions editor at Revell. She creates space for people to be known, nurtured, and challenged through her work, and desires to elevate women of color's voices in the publishing industry. Grace is the coeditor of *Take Heart: 100 Devotions to Seeing God When Life's Not Okay*, coauthor of *Empowered: More of Him for All of You*, and the author of the (in)courage Bible studies *Courageous Influence* and *Create in Me a Heart of Wisdom*. Learn more at gracepcho.com and @gracepcho.

Mary Carver writes and speaks with humor and honesty, encouraging women with truth found in unexpected places. She hosts *The Couch*, a podcast about pop culture and faith, and is the author of *Women of Courage*, *Journey to the Cross*, the (in)courage Bible studies *Courageous Joy* and *Create in Me a Heart of Hope*, as well as a coauthor of *Empowered: More of Him for All of You*. Connect with Mary online at marycarver.com and @marycarver.

A storyteller at heart, **Michele Cushatt** writes and speaks on grit, leadership, and faith in the hard places. A three-time head-and-neck cancer survivor and a mama to children "from hard places," Michele is a (reluctant) expert on pain, trauma, and our deep need for the presence of God exactly where we are. She lives in Colorado with her husband and six children. Learn more at michelecushatt.com.

Kristen Strong, author of *When Change Finds You*, *Back Roads to Belonging*, and *Girl Meets Change*, writes as a friend helping you see a more hopeful view of the difficult change in your life. She and her USAF veteran husband, David, have three children. Kristen would love to connect with you on Instagram @kristenstrong and at kristenstrong.com.

Melissa Zaldivar is an author, speaker, and researcher living near Boston, Massachusetts. She hosts the *Cheer Her On* podcast and is the author of *Kingdom Come* (with a second book on the way!). She holds a master's degree in theology and a bachelor's degree in communications, and you can usually find her in an antique store, leading tours at Orchard House, or walking along the coast. Connect with her at melissa zaldivar.com and @melissazaldivar.

A writer of faith and mysteries, **Patricia Raybon** is an award-winning Colorado author and novelist who writes top-rated books at the daring intersection of faith and race. Her latest release, *All That Is Secret*, is the first of her mystery series set in Denver in the 1920s. She is a contributor for Our Daily Bread and (in)courage. Learn more at patricia raybon.com.

(in)courage welcomes you

to an online community of women who seek Jesus together. Each weekday we meet you right where you are, as one of our thirty writers shares what's going on in her everyday life and how God's right in the middle of it all. They bring their unique experiences—joys and struggles equally—so that you can feel less alone and be empowered by the hope Jesus gives.

Learn more and join the sisterhood at **incourage.me** and connect with us on social media **@incourage**.

Seeking more hope, peace, wisdom, and mercy? We've got you.

This Bible study collection from (in)courage pairs Scripture with personal stories in a way that will ignite your faith and lead you to the full life in Christ that you long for. Packed with solid observation, interpretation, and application of Scripture, plus daily prayers and weekly memory verses, each study will strengthen your relationship with God.